Beat Stress

Alice Muir

D1009698

Teach®
Yourself

Beat Stress

Alice Muir

Hodder Education

338 Euston Road, London NW1 3BH.

Hodder Education is an Hachette UK company

First published in UK 2012 by Hodder Education

First published in US 2012 by The McGraw-Hill Companies, Inc

Copyright © 2012 Alice Muir

The moral rights of the author have been asserted

Database right Hodder Education (makers)

The *Teach Yourself* name is a registered trademark of Hachette UK.

British Library Cataloguing in Publication Data: a catalogue record for this
title is available from the British Library.

Library of Congress Catalog Card Number: on file

10 9 8 7 6 5 4 3 2 1

The publisher has used its best endeavours to ensure that any website
addresses referred to in this book are correct and active at the time of going
to press. However, the publisher and the author have no responsibility for
the websites and can make no guarantee that a site will remain live or that
the content will remain relevant, decent or appropriate.

The publisher has made every effort to mark as such all words which it
believes to be trademarks. The publisher should also like to make it clear
that the presence of a word in the book, whether marked or unmarked, in
no way affects its legal status as a trademark.

Every reasonable effort has been made by the publisher to trace the
copyright holders of material in this book. Any errors or omissions should
be notified in writing to the publisher, who will endeavour to rectify the
situation for any reprints and future editions.

Hachette UK's policy is to use papers that are natural, renewable and
recyclable products and made from wood grown in sustainable forests.
The logging and manufacturing processes are expected to conform to the
environmental regulations of the country of origin.

www.hoddereducation.co.uk

Cover image © Scanrail – Fotolia

Typeset by Cenveo Publisher Services.

Printed in Great Britain by CPI Group (UK) Ltd, Croydon, CR0 4YY.

Also available
in ebook

Contents

Introduction

Welcome to *Teach Yourself Beat Stress*. And be assured, there is so much that you can do to cope better with stress and, ultimately, to 'beat it'. I say 'beat it', because it can seem like you're struggling with an enemy, a powerful and unpredictable enemy, which can scare, confuse and overwhelm you: indeed, it can feel as if some invisible inexplicable opponent has beaten you and taken over your life. Few of us have escaped stress, and I too know what it feels like. But you can get the upper hand again. You can teach yourself to know your enemy, and you can learn how to fight back. And when you do that you will be able to 'Beat Stress'.

You may be surprised to hear that I wrote this introduction last, after finishing writing the book itself. I've always found it easier to do it that way. This may seem a strange idea at first but, if you think about it, it's not easy to introduce something that you haven't even written yet. You need some idea of where you're going, and what kind of book you've produced. And often the book you start off writing bears little resemblance to the end product! I'm definitely finding it so much more straightforward writing this now, with the book all neatly printed up and laid out before me, and the key content and messages already decided, clear and obvious.

But even though it's much easier to write an introduction after finishing the book, somehow I still had trouble actually getting started. Before settling down to write, this very wet July morning in 2012, with my laptop and coffee, I found it absolutely essential to feed the cat. And then I just couldn't leave that drooping plant any longer without a drink of water. And of course, those toys on the floor really begged to be stacked neatly in the toy box. There's just something so off-putting about that blank page staring up at me. Or nowadays, that blank laptop screen. There's something unnerving about the idea of having to write that first word and take that first step. And what is that first sentence going to be? What am I going to say? And there's that looming deadline to meet too, and the thought of my publisher breathing down my neck as it approaches. It can altogether just feel so daunting. But sooner or later I settle down, as I have today, and make those choices, and get started. Before I know it, the screen is no longer blank and scary. It's a work in progress. I'm on my way.

All this has made me think: isn't my experience this morning very like trying to cope with stress? You may really want to do something about it, but there are so many other pressures and so many people competing for your attention, and there is so little time. Or there's too much time, and you just can't find that energy to get yourself moving. And even if you do get round to thinking about it, as I'm sure you have, it's so hard to know what to do. It can be just like my blank page. No idea where to start. So many choices. Everyone seems to have a different angle, different suggestions, persuading and pulling you this way and that. You have no book laid out before you. No guide to show you the way.

However, in the end you really must do something about it as, most of the time, stress simply won't go away by itself. You are worth it, even if you don't feel you are. Take my word for it, as someone with personal experience of stress, and with over 20 years' experience of helping thousands of other people cope better with stress. We all deserve a life that's as stress-free as possible: that's the right of every one of us. And that's what this book is for. It's about showing you a clear pathway, and helping you find the energy and motivation, so that taking that first step to dealing with your stress will become so much easier. In fact, you've already taken your first step. You're reading my introduction. Job done! Now, you're on your way, so don't stop to feed the cat, or water the plants. Now it's time to move on to step two...

1

The truth about stress

This is a book for anyone who wants to know more about stress and how to cope better with it. Any one of us can be affected by stress for one reason or another. Any background, any age, and both men and women can find themselves feeling stressed. Almost everyone has at least had a brush with it. In this chapter, we'll explore what stress is and how this book can help you to deal with it.

Being stressed can be bewildering, confusing and frightening, and it can be very difficult to work out what to do for the best. It can seem impossible to find anyone you can trust enough to talk about it or to help you. And of course, sometimes you can't tell anyone because of what they might think of you. It might even affect your job prospects if they found out about it at work.

What is stress? What brings it on? Who gets stressed? This book will explain what stress is, how it can make you feel, and what you can do about it. Reading a book like this may not be able to remove whatever is making you stressed, but it will give you many, many very practical and straightforward ideas on what you can do to cope far more effectively with that stress. It will also show you ways you might go about deciding if anything can be done about the cause of the stress. Many people feel that they have lost control of their lives, and that they are at the mercy of stress. This book will show you how you can reclaim control over your life.

All through the book there will be lots for you to be involved in. There will be ideas and information to think about, techniques to try, and checklists and questionnaires to work on. So have a small notebook and pencil or pen ready, or a netbook, or laptop. Some different coloured or shaped 'sticky pads' might come in useful too.

That way, you can jot down answers to questionnaires, or make a note of any explanations or techniques you've found particularly helpful, or write down anything that occurs to you as you are reading. Keep your notes somewhere safe, they are just for you, a kind of 'Personal Journal'.

But rest assured, nothing in the book is about having to give the 'correct answers'. It's all about giving you the time and space to think, or try things out in a way that there isn't usually time for. Let's start by finding out how you feel right now.

How do you feel?

Here are five key ideas from this chapter to think about now. They will be discussed later:

1 How often have you felt stressed in the past year or so?

   a Now and then

   b Just once

   c Lots of times

   d Never

   e All the time

   f Don't know

   g Other

2 How does stress make you feel? Try to put this into a few phrases, or as a short list.

3 What sorts of things have stressed you in the past year (choose all that apply)?

   a Not sure

   b Don't know

   c Nothing

   d Work

   e Relationships

    f   Time pressure

    g   Not having a job

    h   Boredom

    i   Family

    j   Poor health

    k   Drugs or alcohol

    l   Money

    m   Neighbours

    n   Other

4 Do you feel you are more likely to become stressed than people you know?

5 How long does your feeling of being stressed generally last for?

    a   I feel stressed all the time

    b   A day or so

    c   A few days

    d   Two or three weeks

    e   A few hours

    f   Months at a time

    g   Don't know

    h   Other

What to expect

Near the beginning of each chapter there will be a short assessment, like the one you've just completed, to give you the chance to rate yourself on how you feel, and to begin thinking about some of the key issues to be discussed in the chapter that follows.

Everything in the book is straightforward and easy to follow, with as little jargon used as possible. This is important as stress tends to make it hard to concentrate. Just move through chapter by chapter at your own pace, or dip in and out of the book to suit your interests. Give yourself enough thinking time, and enough time to absorb the ideas, and try out the suggestions and techniques you'll find throughout the book. This book won't provide an overnight miracle, but what you'll read will help you to overcome your stress, provided you start to put it into action.

Remember this

For simplicity, your notebook (or other method of recording material from this book) will be referred to as your Personal Journal.

OPTIONAL EXTRAS

You'll also find there are 'Optional extras' for each chapter, which you'll find in Appendix 1 and Appendix 2 at the back of the book. If you want to learn more about the topics in a particular chapter, you'll find 'add-ons' such as more techniques and activities to try, or helpful case studies to read, or particularly useful websites to check out on the internet. You'll find an asterisk * when there are Optional extras about the topic you're reading about.

The stress puzzle

We all hear so much about stress. Hardly a day goes by without a story in the newspaper or a magazine, or a discussion on a TV programme. So, what do you already know about stress?

1 We all think we know what stress is. So have a shot at jotting down an answer to the question 'What is stress?'

2 How easy/difficult did you find this to do and why?

3 Think about people you know who have been stressed, or your own experiences of stress. Now make up a list of as many signs

and symptoms of stress which you can think of under these three general headings (some of these overlap; don't worry about this):

a Physical symptoms

b Emotions/mind/thinking

c Behaviour.

4 Do you think more men or more women have problems coping with stress? Why do you think this might be?

5 Is there a particular age group you think is more likely to have difficulties with stress, or do you feel that it may affect all ages equally?

Try it now

Top to toe:
1 Read what to do first, then try it with your eyes closed.
2 Starting with your toes, and moving mentally through your body, slowly check for any tension. Take around a minute, and end with the top of your head.
3 Now take in a deep breath, and as you sigh it back out, release any tension you found. Then take another deep breath, and sigh out any tension that didn't disappear with your first breath.

WHAT IS STRESS?

It's difficult to clearly explain what stress is because, in everyday language, the word 'stress' is used in two quite different ways:

1 In everyday speech, we talk about financial worries, or relationship problems, or difficulties at work as 'stress'. In other words, stress is outside pressures or circumstances. You often hear the phrase 'he was under a lot of stress'.

2 But what you feel or experience in such situations is also described as stress. You feel stressed! So 'stress' is also used to describe our internal world.

We need to understand both of these sides to stress, if we want to be able to deal with it. We need to know about these outside pressures, and we need to know about the effects they have on people. To make this easier these two important parts of stress are better described in this way:

Remember this

How your mind and body feel when you are stressed = STRESS

↕

Situation/s you find stressful = STRESSOR/S.

When we feel stressed, the automatic part of our nervous system becomes energized, or aroused. That's the part of the nervous system which keeps us breathing and our heart beating automatically, without us having to think about it. This arousal is a necessary part of our biological make-up, and evolved in our caveman ancestors as a mechanism which prepared them to cope *physically* with whatever situation they might experience, from hunting, to gathering food, to sitting around the fire. The level of arousal would be just right.

So if our ancestors came upon something life-threatening and dangerous, like a snarling sabre-toothed tiger, or hissing snake, or aggressive members of another tribe, this instant automatic arousal prepared them to either 'fight', or 'flee' as fast as they could. Arousal became set on maximum to increase the chance of survival. This all happens instantly, and automatically, because if our ancestors had taken time to think about it, it would have been too late. Breathing and thinking processes speed up, the heart beats faster to take more blood and oxygen to the muscles, which become taut and ready for action, blood sugar levels rise to give rapid energy, increased amounts of adrenalin are produced, and so on. All in the blink of an eye, to prepare us for instant and effective action, to save our lives, or that of a loved one.

WHAT'S ALL THE FUSS ABOUT THEN?

In terms of evolution, development of the automatic nervous system is relatively recent. Our bodies react in exactly the same way today, in the 21st-century high street, supermarket or office block as they did in the cave. But in our modern world, we don't just feel threatened by *physically* dangerous situations. We can feel threatened and in danger from an angry neighbour, or a pile of bills falling on the mat. And we can't solve problems like these by physically fighting with our work colleagues, or running away from an upsetting text or e-mail, much as we might want to. So in today's world there is seldom a *physical* outlet for the ancient 'fight or flight' reaction, and the major bodily changes it generates. These have no outlet, leaving you feeling very strange indeed:

▶ Sitting at your desk with a racing heart, thinking you're having a heart attack.

▶ Driving to work with a tense, arched back.

▶ Holding your coffee cup with a vice-like grip.

▶ Tired all the time because your blood sugar is burning off too quickly and then falling.

▶ Prone to moods and angry outbursts, and an inability to make the simplest decision as your blood sugar can suddenly fall too low.

▶ Feeling spaced out on the train home from work, because you're breathing a little too fast, and your body's delicate chemical balance is out of sorts.

▶ Finding nail marks in your palms after talking to your child's teacher at parents' night.

▶ Discovering your jaw and teeth are clamped shut whilst in the queue at the supermarket.

▶ No appetite, or indigestion, because your stomach has shut down to allow all hands to be on deck to 'fight' or 'flee'.

▶ Can't concentrate in meetings because your mind feels in fast-forward mode, and is jumping all over the place.

▶ Muscles becoming painful in the evenings as they've been tense most of the day for no reason.

Mythbuster

We're already talking about stress as a problem, and the experience of stress as a negative and unwanted one. But some people will tell you that a little stress is good for you. This is a myth. Yes, we all need some positive challenge in our lives in order to perform at our best, but this is better thought of as useful stimulation, rather than stress. Saying a little stress is good for you is like saying don't be knocked down by a full-sized bus, but if it's a little mini-bus then it would do you good. Not.

The International Stress Management Society UK (ISMA^UK) explains stress as (2012):

> 'The adverse reaction people have to excessive pressures or other types of demand placed on them.'

Those pressures may come from many differing sources and when their combined effect is overwhelming, stress occurs. This means that stress is not good for you. Stress is an unhealthy state of body or mind or both.

STRESS IS NORMAL

Stress is a normal human response. It's normal in the sense that the stress response itself isn't an illness or a disease. We've already seen that it's a normal human reaction, designed to keep us safe from physical danger, and shared with most animals. Everyone has this automatic response to danger, which in our ancestors would occur for a few seconds or minutes, very occasionally, usually if there was a snake, wild animal or other physical threat to be dealt with quickly. When we experience stress, there is in fact nothing physically wrong with us.

Even today, the stress response still keeps us safe from physical danger. If you're on your mobile phone, and take a step into the road without thinking, and then see a heavy lorry bearing down on you, it's the ancient stress response that will make you step back again swiftly and without thinking. It's the same response that is responsible for those people who find the superhuman strength to lift a car which has pinned down a loved one, or rescue a child from a burning building.

It's when the 'everyday' stress reaction occurs too severely, too often, or if it becomes long-term, that a range of other physical or psychological illness and conditions can be produced. There will be more on this in Chapter 2.

Remember this

'Stress' has become a problem for modern men and women because the stress response is being produced too often, and when we are in 'psychological', rather than physical danger. Examples would be when the bills are piling up, we have an argument with a loved one, or a deadline approaches too quickly for us at work. Our bodies weren't designed for the stress response to occur in this way, especially without a physical outlet for the major bodily changes it brings. This can leave you feeling confused, scared and miserable, and will make you feel ill, even though you aren't actually ill.

ARE WE MORE STRESSED THAN 20 YEARS AGO?

It's easy to think of periods in human history, which, on the face of it, would appear to have been more stressful than today. Typical examples would be times of famine, war, disease or desperate poverty. With the progress that has been made in eradicating disease and absolute poverty in Western societies, should there not be less stress nowadays instead of more? Though we cannot be sure, the most likely answer is no, we are probably more stressed in the West today than in most historical periods.

The main reason for this is the huge increase in psychological stressors, brought about by today's sophisticated, high-speed, non-stop global existence. But there are other reasons too:

▶ In the past, most periods of stress would be due to war or famine, and would be short and infrequent, alternating with long periods of relative peace and prosperity.

▶ Also, without a 24-hour news service, only those directly involved would be aware of a stressor such as fighting, or a plague, and be affected by it.

▶ Today's global village allows us all to be fully aware of the desperate situations experienced by people at the other end of the country, or the other side of the world, and to see and hear what is happening in war zones. This makes many people feel stressed by proxy.

▶ During the two major and lengthy world wars of the 20th century, or the great Depression of the 1930s, people had a sense of being in it together. This had the effect of reducing the adverse effects of a time of great stress considerably. Feeling you are alone with a stressor can make its effects much stronger.

▶ Current industrial Western society emphasizes the importance of the independent individual, exercising choice and making decisions in a world where material success matters. This automatically places continuous stress on people to strive for material success: the rat race, in other words, with its unrelenting time pressure and constant change.

▶ Stress appears to be an unavoidable by-product of 21st century life in a Western-style society.

Try it now

Breathe easy

1 Place a flat hand gently on your tummy. You can do this in any position, and anywhere. No one will notice.
2 Now breathe in gently through your nose to a count of 1-2-3-4, making sure to let your tummy rise, then as you breathe out gently, count 1-2-3-4-5.
3 Repeat up to five times.

WHAT ABOUT THE REST OF THE WORLD?

There are undoubtedly numerous stressors in the West, but a recent survey of 6,500 women in 21 countries, including the UK and USA, found that stress in the developing countries, such as India, Mexico, Russia and China is even greater. The survey was completed in 2011 by the consumer and media research company Nielsen, and it found that women in the developing countries are more stressed than women in the West. Women in India were the most stressed of all, in terms of feeling time pressure, lack of time to relax, and feeling overworked most of the time.

Nielsen puts this down to financial pressures, with women in India saying they were unlikely to have anything left after paying for necessities. Nielsen takes this financial argument on to explain the overall findings that what were called 'daughters' (average age 30) were most stressed, 'mothers' (average age 47) a bit less so, and 'grandmothers' (average age 67) least stressed, because of increasing financial security and work/life balance.

Another major global survey, completed by the Kenexa High Performance Institute, focussed on 60,000 'employees' in Brazil, China, Germany, India, the UK, and the USA. This reported in 2012, that UK workers were the most stressed of the six countries, with 35 per cent being exposed to unreasonable levels of stress at work. However, the levels in Brazil, Germany and the USA weren't far behind.

Country	Percentage of employees stressed in 2012
UK	35 (up 10% since 2008)
Brazil	34
Germany	33
USA	32
China	17
India	17

HIGH AND LOW-STRESS OCCUPATIONS
CareerCast is an American organization, which keeps data on the stress associated with various careers. In 2012, they studied 100 occupations, and ranked their experience of stress based on 11 factors including: deadlines, physical demands, environmental conditions, and being in the public eye. Here are their ten most stressful and ten least stressful jobs:

Ten most stressful jobs in 2012	Ten least stressful jobs in 2012
1 Enlisted soldier	1 Medical records technician
2 Firefighter	2 Jeweller
3 Airline pilot	3 Hair Stylist
4 Military General	4 Dressmaker/Tailor
5 Police Officer	5 Medical laboratory technician
6 Event Co-ordinator	6 Audiologist
7 Public Relations Executive	7 Precision assembler
8 Senior Corporate Executive	8 Dietician
9 Photojournalist	9 Furniture upholsterer
10 Taxi Driver	10 Electrical technician

In 2005, a research project headed by C.T. Millet identified that in the UK, the seven most stressful occupations were:

1 ambulance service

2 teaching

3 social services

4 customer services – call centres

5 prison officers

6 clerical and administration

7 police

The group also found that within the same occupational setting, there were interesting role differences, such as police officers and classroom teachers being more stressed than their senior colleagues. They flagged up the idea that the 'emotional' nature of work is an important factor in creating stress, with 'emotional work' meaning a role which includes significant amounts of direct interaction with clients who commonly show their emotions.

HOW MANY PEOPLE ARE STRESSED?

Few would disagree that stress in the UK has increased in recent decades. Doctors, employers and health and welfare staff would probably agree that stress has been steadily rising for the past 50–60 years. Stress is not easy to pin down, and reports and measures are always going to be at least one or two years out-of-date by the time they appear, but here is some very recent evidence:

▶ The Health and Safety Executive (HSE) estimate that in 2011, 10.8 million working days were lost through stress, anxiety or depression, caused or made worse by stress.

▶ In their 2011 Absence Management Survey, produced in partnership with Simplyhealth, the Chartered Institute of Personnel and Development (CIPD) found that stress was the most common reason for long-term sickness absence, both for manual and non-manual employees.

MIND reported in 2011 that British businesses lose an estimated £26 billion each year in sickness absence and lost productivity. With greater awareness and mental health support, one third of these costs could be saved – £8 billion a year.

The HSE figures break down to show that in 2011, more women than men were affected, and those aged 45–54, whether men or women, were most at risk. The age breakdown currently varies year on year, and there is evidence of younger people becoming increasingly affected depending on the economic situation.

	Those reporting being affected by stress, anxiety or depression related to work. Millions of days off in 2011.
Of the entire working population	10.8
Men	4.9
Women	5.9
TOTAL	10.8
Age 16-34	2.5
Age 35-44	2.6
Age 45-54	3.8
Age 55 and over	1.9
TOTAL	10.8

FIVE EASY STEPS TO FIND HOW STRESSED YOU ARE

▶ Step one:

Just for a few moments, take time to think about your own life just now, and about the week that has just gone. In your notebook, list everything you can think of which is going on in your life and which could be causing you unhelpful stress at the moment. It helps if you think about family, work, relationships, weather, events, daily hassles, travel, cars, money, your home, and so on. List these 'stressors' in any order, down the left-hand side of a page. Take your time, and allow yourself to become aware of all stressors in your life.

↓

▶ **Step two:**

Now go back through your list, and down the right-hand side of the same page, rate each on a scale of 1–10 (10 being maximum stress you can imagine) of how stressful it is for you just now. Be HONEST.

▶ **Step three:**

Now add all these scores up to give your Current Stress. This puts a figure on the potential for unhelpful stress in your life right now. Write this number down at the bottom of your list of numbers, just like your total bill in a restaurant.

▶ **Step four:**

Bear in mind that the ideal score here would be zero, as we are clearly thinking about unhelpful stress. As explained earlier, it is better to think that all stress is unhelpful, and that the popular idea of there being 'useful stress', to spur us on to greater things, is better thought of as 'challenge' or 'stimulation', which we all need in life. There is no maximum score!

▶ **Step five:**

Now go back to the page you were working on, and using the scale below, rate your personal vulnerability to stress. How likely are you, as a person, to experience stress in reaction to certain circumstances or events. Be honest. Write this number down directly underneath your answer to the previous question. Nearly there!

VULNERABILITY	
Average vulnerability	0
Slightly vulnerable	2
Moderately vulnerable	3
Very vulnerable	4

Now add these last two numbers together – that is add your CURRENT STRESS to your VULNERABILITY to find out your TOTAL STRESS RATING.

| CURRENT STRESS | + | VULNERABILITY | = | TOTAL STRESS RATING |

Remember that ideally this total should be zero. We all function most efficiently if we have no stress. And sadly, there is probably no maximum score. A low score would be anything from 0 to 5, medium from 6–10, high from 11–20, and very high, 21 and above. Many people these days will find they have a low to medium score. If your score is higher than you would like, this book will help you do something about that.

WE ARE ALL DIFFERENT

Stress is not something which just comes out of the blue, from outside of us. It can feel that way, but it's not. It's not like a shower of rain, which wets each of us equally. Some of us are drenched, but some of us remain dry, even if we get caught in the same shower of stress. You see, there are many situations one person will experience as stressful, whilst another feels it as a challenge, or even as an everyday event; public speaking, car racing, writing a report, amateur dramatics, abseiling, city driving or visiting the dentist are just a few examples. Just as no two people look alike or have identical personalities, we all experience stress differently, and in response to different stressors.

Remember this

How we perceive or assess a situation will decide whether or not we feel stressed by it. So stress is the outcome of not one but two factors – it depends on the person, and it depends on the situation in which they find themselves.

An important figure in introducing this idea was psychologist Richard Lazarus, who in 1952 explained that a person's assessment of the situation will decide whether they experience stress or not. This assessment will depend on the individual's personality and previous experience. We all assess situations day in, day out, sometimes actively, sometimes without really thinking about it. It's all just part of our daily experience of life. But whatever the cause of our stress, we still have a choice – to lie down to it or fight back.

So in most day-to-day situations, how someone appraises a situation largely determines whether or not they will experience stress. This needn't be a conscious process. It can feel completely unthinking and automatic. And this is very much down to the three Ps: our physical make-up, personality and previous experience.

Remember though, no one is immune to stress. All it takes is for the right buttons to be pressed, and it can happen to anyone. And this doesn't mean that you can't do something to 'cushion' yourself from these various effects, and improve your coping skills. Or, in terms of my previous 'shower of stress' metaphor, you should always carry an umbrella.

DIFFERENT TYPES OF STRESS

The stress expert, Professor Hans Selye famously said in 1973, 'Everybody knows what stress is and nobody knows what it is.' This puts it particularly well. We all have an intuitive feel for what it is, but have difficulty in putting that into words.

In 1946, Professor Selye described three stages in reacting, or adapting, to the stressors we can meet in our lives. These are still a useful concept over 60 years later. In stage one, the alarm is set off by any stressor, and the body gets ready to deal with this. In stage two the body attempts to resist the stressor, and if it is successfully achieved, there will be a return to some sort of equilibrium. In other words all will return to normal. If the body's attempt at resistance does not deal with the stressor, or if the stressor persists for too long, the third stage, that of exhaustion, will be reached.

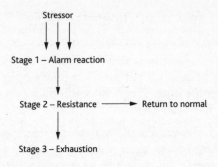

Stressor

Stage 1 – Alarm reaction

Stage 2 – Resistance ⟶ Return to normal

Stage 3 – Exhaustion

Selye's way of looking at stress still has practical implications for how we experience it today.

Stress can come in a short, sharp or acute burst. Maybe a job interview, a house move, or an exam. We psyche ourselves up for this, get through it, and then heave a sigh of relief when it's over, and get back to normal, with no harm done.

Or, stress can be long-lasting, seeming to go on and on, such as might happen to a carer, or in a relationship which isn't working, or if you have a stressful job. Or stress can be intermittent, sometimes there sometimes not, depending on what's going on in your life. Either way, if this goes on for too long, exhaustion results. This is what is sometimes described as 'burnout', which can take months or more to recover from.

Case study

Doreen has been caring for her mother, who is 75 and has dementia, in her own home for three years. She has no other family and feels it is her responsibility anyway. It was quite stressful at first, but then Doreen seemed to just get used to it. But lately she feels drained, empty inside, and tired all the time, and often feels tense and irritable, with a tendency to snap at her mother which she'd never experienced before. She's also had several colds this last six months, as well as the winter vomiting virus.

Comment: Ethel has reached Selye's third stage, and is experiencing the outcome of long-term stress, and possible burnout. She's tense, exhausted and her immune system is well below par. She needs time to recover, and should see her doctor about how this can be organized.

How to tell if you're stressed*

If you are stressed you will notice signs and symptoms. Everyone does. These are the effects of increased autonomic nervous system (ANS) arousal with no outlet. There are many effects of stress because, as shown earlier, the ANS underlies everything the body does. Although no list can be complete, the diagram below shows the common symptoms which many people who suffer from stress will recognize. Perhaps you could tick or make a note of those which you've experienced. You'll find more on this in Optional extras (Appendix 1).

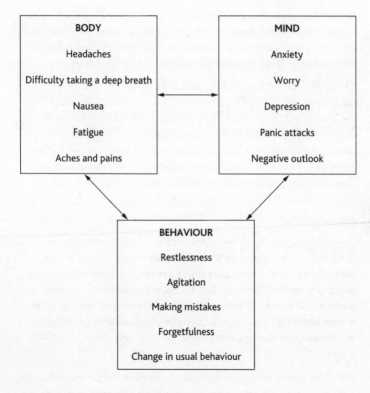

BODY

Headaches

Difficulty taking a deep breath

Nausea

Fatigue

Aches and pains

MIND

Anxiety

Worry

Depression

Panic attacks

Negative outlook

BEHAVIOUR

Restlessness

Agitation

Making mistakes

Forgetfulness

Change in usual behaviour

Introducing stress management

Up until early in the 20th century, many hundreds of brave soldiers were shot for cowardice, or disobeying orders, or for desertion, when they refused to go into action against the enemy, or refusing orders to go 'over the top' of the notorious World War I trenches. The award winning novel *Birdsong*, by Sebastian Faulks (1993), gives some idea of what life in the trenches was like. Most, if not all of these soldiers were in fact experiencing a highly distressing condition which interfered markedly with their thinking processes and behaviour. Many of these men, or their families, have only recently received pardons and an apology for their appalling treatment.

Stress management as we know it today probably had its roots in the early 1900s, when it was realized that most of these men had developed a condition known as 'shell shock', especially after serving in the trenches on the front line. In these early days, shell shock was assumed to be a neurological dysfunction resulting from brain damage caused by the sound of exploding shells. This was assumed to be the reason for many men becoming so ill, that they could no longer face combat.

During World War II, this condition came to be thought of as more of an emotional breakdown caused by the 'stress' of combat, rather than as a physical condition. Today, we're all familiar with the term 'combat stress' and what it can mean for those affected. It is also sometimes described as 'battle fatigue' or 'war neurosis', and its effects can still be felt many years later. Some never fully recover.

After World War II ended in 1945, medics, psychologists, psychiatrists and other professionals began to suspect that many situations in everyday life could also cause similar effects to battle fatigue. For example, being assaulted or raped, being involved in a serious car accident or house-fire, or being subjected to years of domestic abuse.

This idea is now widely accepted to be the case. More recently, with an increase in armed conflict involving Western countries, increasing attention has been paid to the true nature of battle fatigue, now termed post-traumatic stress syndrome, or PTSD, which is now recognized to occur not just in response to battle, but to a wide range of traumatic events, such as accidents, disasters or abuse. There will be more about PTSD in Chapter 2.

The resulting interest by the military in training men to manage stress, and a new general emphasis on personal development, gave rise to the development of stress management on a much wider platform than just the armed forces from the 1950s onwards.

Try it now

Tension release

In your own time, breathe in slowly, and as you do this, silently check over your entire body for any unwanted tension in your muscles. Check your scalp, face, shoulders, hands, back, chest, stomach, legs, feet... just notice where there is extra unwanted tension in your body.

Then, with your next breath out, quietly release the tension you found.

Repeat.

WHAT CAN YOU DO IF YOU'RE STRESSED?

Stress is what we feel when there is an unnecessary increase in autonomic arousal, bringing about unwelcome and out of place physical and mental changes. So the main aim when treating stress is to reduce this autonomic arousal and the symptoms it brings about. Chapter 2 will go in to this in much more detail, and other chapters will pick up on this too, but for now we will simply list the main areas which have been found to have this effect:

▶ Reducing stress

Clearly the simplest strategy would be to do something about the cause of the stress – your stressors. This may not always be possible, but sometimes specialist advice and a lot of thought can help you to make personal decisions which will help to resolve or reduce one or all of your stressors.

▶ Advice, understanding, listening and support

Feeling isolated and alone only exacerbates stress. But if you understand your problems better, you are in with a chance of dealing with them. Knowing there's an objective sounding board to listen and not judge can be an immense support too. Sometimes just understanding what stress is and how it affects your body can be a huge relief.

▶ Relaxation exercises

Excess ANS arousal produces more tension than you need for everyday tasks. There's a very wide range of relaxation techniques for both body and mind, some taking only moments, and there is usually something to suit everyone.

▶ Breathing

Simple breathing exercises can quickly restore normal breathing patterns and reduce the severity of symptoms. This can be surprisingly effective.

▶ Lifestyle change

The right changes can have a major cushioning effect and impact on stress levels. Taking regular breaks and more exercise for example, can be of tremendous benefit, perhaps more than you can imagine.

▶ Sorting out priorities and finding regular support

Sorting out priorities, deciding what's really important, and seeking social and other support can be an enormous help.

▶ Thinking habits

The way we habitually think about life can encourage or inhibit stress. The chronic negative thinker, or the person who sets standards which are too high for themselves, can produce their own stress. Raising awareness of these and other unhelpful thinking habits, and making changes to them, can yield great improvements. Some of these may surprise you.

Remember this

Although there is a huge choice of stress management techniques, research and experience would suggest that the most powerful and effective way to manage stress for most people involves a combination of:

▶ some form of relaxation

▶ breathing exercises of some kind

▶ gaining an understanding about the causes of stress and how it can affect the body and mind.

SIX STEPS TO FIND WHAT IS STRESSING YOU

Now that you're more familiar with stress and what it is, let's look at what sorts of situations cause stress, and also the kinds of stressors which are affecting you personally just now.

Step one:
Find a small pad of sticky notes (or even better, three in different colours or shapes), some small dot or star stickers, and a large (A4 or bigger) piece of blank paper. A large piece of brown wrapping paper, on the wall is good. Draw a rough circle about the size of a 10 pence piece in the centre of the paper. This is you.

Step two:
Think about the country you live in, and then think about the part of the country where you spend most of your time. What do you feel are the main causes of stress there? Think as broadly as you can. Write one on each sticky, and stick these on the sheet around YOU, placing those which you feel affect you most, nearest to you. Examples might be unemployment, difficult neighbours, lack of leisure facilities, bad weather, poor schools.

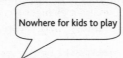

Step three:
Now think about the country you live in as a whole, are there any other causes you could now add (using a second shape or colour of sticky note if you have these)? Examples for the UK might be cut-backs, poor health, family or relationship problems, drug or alcohol abuse.

Step four:
Now think in detail about workplace stress. Make sticky notes (third colour) for some of the reasons people might be stressed in their workplace.

Step five:
Now look over all the sticky notes you've made and put a cross (or a star or dot sticker if you have any) on those which you feel are affecting you right now.

Step six:
Now go back to those with crosses/stars, and rate how much stress they are causing you at the moment. Use a scale of 1–10, 1 being the minimum and 10 being maximum stress. You should now have a picture of your stress.

STRESS IS ALL AROUND US*

Are your days entirely ruled by the clock, with so much to be squeezed into too little time? Are you continually juggling home life around work? Or maybe there's almost nowhere and no time you can't be contacted by mobile phones, pagers or e-mail. All of this, and everything else that goes with life in the early 21st century, is a heavy burden for a body which was skilfully designed over countless centuries for the slow pace of the Stone Age.

You'll find more stories of people experiencing stress in the Optional extras for Chapter 1 in Appendix 1 at the back of the book. In the meantime, here are just some of the stressors we cope with every day.

STRESS CAN ALSO COME FROM 'GOOD' EVENTS

It's not only the negative events of life which are stressful. Even events which are very welcome can cause stress. This is because happy events, such as a wedding, or a much wanted promotion, new house or baby will involve a number of factors such as financial worries, a feeling of lack of control, or time pressure, all of which can cause stress. Most of us would worry about an extension that's taking forever to build, or a baby that won't stop crying, or not being able to sell our current home when the next

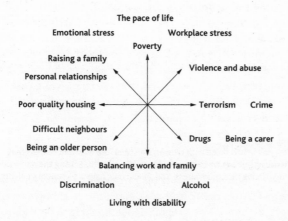

one is all set up and ready to go. Even arranging a wedding or a holiday involves time pressure to make sure it will all be alright on the day, and worrying about whether you can afford it, or what might go wrong unexpectedly. The other thing is that most positive life events involve change, and change, even good change, is stressful too.

WORKPLACE STRESS

Workplace stress is being talked about and recognized more and more. The importance of 'job satisfaction' as referred to so aptly by US President Roosevelt in 1903, has definitely given way a century later, to concerns about long hours, down-sizing, short-term contracts, new methods of working, and organizational change. The unemployed are stressed because they don't have a job, and the workforce is stressed because they do.

According to the Chartered Institute of Personnel and Development (CIPD) in their 2011 Absence Management Survey, produced in partnership with Simplyhealth, the main cause of stress in the public sector was organizational change and restructuring.

There is no magic wand which will make workplace stress just disappear. It is largely an outcome of the nature of Britain and other developed countries in the second decade of the 21st century. For many people, there is little they can do, except cushion themselves from its effects. Many employers are also at a loss to know what to do, and receive mixed messages about stress and the workforce from different sources. Specific skills for employers, the self-employed, and the employee to use to manage workplace stress will be suggested throughout the book, and especially in Chapters 2, 3, 4, 12 and 13.

ATTITUDES TO STRESS
Sometimes the worst thing about feeling stressed is being concerned about what other people are going to think. How will friends and family react? And what about the neighbours or work colleagues? There is still a stigma about anything to do with mental health, but stress is becoming more accepted year by year.

But sometimes it's a person's own attitude that can be the problem. Sometimes people just won't admit or recognize that they are stressed. So it's not just about other people's attitudes, it's also about our own too.

Case study
Norman is a 52-year-old senior executive I first met some years ago, who has always prided himself on a job well done. He is a proud man who has worked hard to get where he is today. Over the years he has come across people who had problems with stress, and was always of the mind that they just needed to give themselves a shake, and show more strength, show more backbone. But in the past five years, his company has downsized and re-organized several times, meaning an increased and ever-changing workload for Norman, often involving new

computer technology, which he has always felt somewhat wary of, and has never quite come to grips with. In the past few months, he has been experiencing chronic neck pain and severe headaches which the doctor says might be caused by stress. His wife has also noticed that he is not sleeping well, and has become quite irritable at home. Norman has scoffed at the doctor's suggestion that he might be stressed, but his wife is not so sure. Use your Personal Journal to jot down your thoughts about these questions:

▶ Why do you think Norman denies that he is stressed?

▶ What makes Norman think that stressed people 'need to give themselves a shake'?

▶ Do you think this is a commonly held view? Why should that be?

▶ What do you think of this view of stress?

▶ How is this view likely to affect Norman's motivation to do something about his stress?

▶ Who do you think is most likely to be able to persuade him to do something about his stress? Why?

▶ What do you think those closest to you think about stressed people?

▶ What effect does this have on you?

▶ Is there anyone else whose attitude might affect you (family, work colleagues, boss, etc.)?

▶ How do you think you might deal with this?

▶ Who do you find is supportive towards your problem with stress? Make and keep a list of their names (if any) in your Journal.

Many people are often reluctant to admit they feel stressed. Or they avoid seeking help because it can be perceived as a sign of weakness. Others genuinely don't believe that they are stressed, even when told this by their doctor. That's something which happens to weak people, not to them. And anyway, even if they are stressed, what else is there to do but just get on with it. The stress is there, and can't be changed so what other alternative do they have?

And then of course there is the popular misconception that all a stressed person has to do is give themselves a shake or pull themselves together. If it were that easy, wouldn't every stressed person have done that by now? In fact this is what most stressed people are constantly trying to do – but it just doesn't work. Much of the physical tension associated with stress is an outcome of desperately trying to hold yourself together and stay in control.

Why take the trouble to beat stress?

Because you can! Because you owe it to yourself. Because you can be more rounded, better adjusted, more comfortable and happier. Not just you, but everyone around you will feel happier and more content. You can become more efficient in your work and more ambitious for progression and success. If you have some motivation, some ambition to achieve more than you are, then you can and you will do it. And it isn't as difficult as you think it will be. It's all about knowing how.

Remember this

There is a wealth of helpful information and tried and tested methods to tackle stress in this book. As you go from chapter to chapter, or dip in here and there, don't just skip the activities and techniques – give them a try, and you'll learn so much more that will help you. Stress management is a very practical and individual thing; it's not a blanket programme for all. Be selective and choose what works best for you, and will suit you and your lifestyle and personality best.

ONE CHANGE AT A TIME

Don't be tempted to make too many changes all at once, even if you're all set, and really keen to do something about stress. Only make one change at a time if you want it to last. Only build one new skill in to your life at a time. Trying to change too much all at once is itself going to add to tension and stress. As in learning anything new, it's best to take one careful step at a time, make sure you have learned and established that, and then move on to the next. You will get there more quickly and more surely in the end. Those around you also need time to adjust to the new you!

Focus points

1. Stress is defined here as the experience of high autonomic nervous system (ANS) arousal for which there is no outlet in the modern world.

2. Stress therefore produces a wide range of physical, psychological and behavioural symptoms.

3. Stress appears to be on the increase, and can play a part in causing a range of physical and psychological conditions.

4. A range of straightforward and effective techniques can be used for coping better with stress.

5. An individual's total stress is a combination of their life stress and their workplace stress, and some people are more vulnerable to stress than others through no fault of their own.

2

What you need to know about coping with stress

In this chapter, you'll discover the many ways in which stress can affect you. You'll also learn different ways of coping with stress.

The story so far

Stress affects millions of people. There are no magic pills to take, and common sense doesn't have too much to offer either for coping with stress. What this book can do is provide a reliable explanation of what is happening to you when you are stressed, and describe effective and straightforward things you can do to feel better. This book is not a prescription, but it's just as important as one.

People feel stressed when there is a feeling of unwanted pressure because there are things going on in their lives which make them feel one or more of these:

▶ that they can't cope as well as they want to

▶ that they can't cope at all

▶ threatened

▶ trapped

▶ dissatisfied or unhappy

▶ unsure or unfamiliar

▶ overwhelmed.

Depending on the particular circumstances, stress like this can be short-lasting, or go on for months or even years. Stress causes a range of unpleasant symptoms, which can undermine overall health and wellbeing.

How do you feel?

Here are five key ideas from this chapter to think about now. They will be discussed later:

1 Which of these have you tried to help you cope with stress (choose any that apply)?

   a Time off work

   b Prescribed medication

   c Non-prescription medication or health foods

d   Yoga

e   Aromatherapy

f   Reflexology

g   Counselling

h   Coaching

i   Massage

j   Sport

k   Breathing techniques

l   Acupuncture

m   Hypnosis

n   Positive thinking

o   Music

p   Gardening

q   Dancing

r   Talking to friends

s   Alcohol

t   Other

2   For each one chosen in Question 1, give it a score out of 10 as to how effective it was.

3   Why did you choose these (select all that apply)?

a   Not sure

b   Doctor suggested

c   Friend suggested

d   Partner suggested

e   Found on the internet

f   Thought it might work

g Easy answer

h Read in a magazine

i Saw on television

j Last resort

k It just looked good

l It was quick or easy

m Other reason/s – what are these?

4 Are you aware of any health problems you have which you think are caused primarily by stress?

5 Are you aware of any health problems you have which you think are being made worse by stress?

A general approach to coping with stress

Knowing how to deal with stress does not come naturally to most people. There's no reason why it should. We haven't been designed for this particular scenario. There is a tendency to use the kind of coping strategies which only make matters worse. In fact, what we do automatically or through common sense can often be counter-productive. For example, people might deny they have a problem, or take it all out on someone else, or work harder and for longer with no breaks. None of this will help. All this will do is intensify their stress, damage their health and wellbeing, and cause distress to those around them. There's more on recognizing unhelpful strategies in Chapter 3.

Although most people are well informed about the existence of stress, they are often unsure about how best to deal with it. Everyone seems to have an angle on stress. There are frequent articles in the press, and on the internet, and regular television documentaries, and they all offer the solution. But these solutions are all different. So how do you choose from all these options? What people who are trying to cope with stress need is clear and reliable advice from a dependable source. This book is that trustworthy source of straightforward advice. Strategies for managing stress which research has found to be effective are set out here.

FOUR LINES OF ATTACK TO BEAT STRESS

A broad range of strategies and techniques for coping better with stress has now been clearly established, and shown to be effective through decades of wide-ranging research. Generally speaking, stress management techniques fall into four types or categories, or lines of attack, though there is inevitably some overlap:

1 Improve understanding of stress.

2 Remove or reduce the cause of the stress.

3 Cushion the effects of stress to dampen down the body's response.

4 Change how the person sees the situation.

How these four lines of attack can work together is shown here. The most effective way to beat stress is to advance step by step on all four fronts.

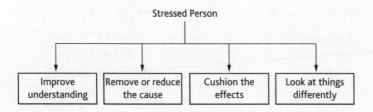

Stressed Person

| Improve understanding | Remove or reduce the cause | Cushion the effects | Look at things differently |

► 1 Improve understanding about stress

Understanding what stress does to your body is so important. This aspect of managing stress is often underrated, and may sometimes not even be included in books, or stress management courses of treatment. However, it can be a crucial component. Armed with newly found understanding, you can escape the vicious circle, whereby more stress is built on top of the original stress through anxiety about the symptoms themselves. Severe headaches, poor concentration, palpitations, dizziness, and chest pain, can all be brought on by stress, but if you don't know that, you'll imagine the worst – but these still need to be checked out.

A panic attack is a good example of the power of understanding. A panic attack is a very common outcome of stress. Knowing what is happening turns an unpredictable and frightening attack into an understandable and normal reaction which you can deal with. There will be more on panic attacks and how to deal with them in Chapter 8.

▶ 2 Remove or reduce the cause

At its most simplistic, all we should need to do to manage our stress is simply remove the cause of it, or at least try to reduce it in some way. Move away from the noisy neighbours, change job, earn more money to pay off the debt, and so on. But we all know it isn't as easy as that. Most of today's stressors are complex, and eliminating them is sometimes very difficult, and often impossible.

However, that said, a first step in managing stress would still have to be an attempt to remove or diminish the cause. Taking specialist advice can help you decide whether anything can realistically be done. There is an abundance of support groups and advisory bodies available today for people to consult for expert advice on their particular problem, and this can be greatly beneficial.

Unfortunately, it is often today's hectic everyday lifestyle which is stressful. Or sometimes the cause of the stress lies within the person themselves. Their personality, nervous system or some other characteristics might increase their vulnerability to stress. Taken together, this means that much of today's stress is unavoidable. The next best thing is to cushion yourself from its effects, and build up your resilience to future stressors. This is what most people have to do and it can be very effective.

▶ 3 Cushion yourself and build resilience

This book will look at various ways of doing this. It's not a magic cure, but can go some way to making life bearable and even enjoyable again. Cushioning can even help to resolve the cause of stress. For example, better time management may help with a heavy workload. Because stress is essentially unnecessary autonomic arousal, the techniques used for cushioning are largely those which reduce autonomic arousal. They are based on a range of well-tried behavioural and psychological techniques including:

Relaxation

There are all sorts of ways to relax. It's down to personal preferences. The important thing is to allow your body to slow down and completely relax at least once every day for at least ten minutes; a lazy bath, a walk, visiting friends, music, yoga, sport, a facial, and so on. Relaxation exercises can help here, because you can usually fit them into your day, and they are also helpful to use to keep stress under control in problem situations. Learning a way of releasing tension and relaxing quickly, within a few seconds, will also open the door to feeling more in control, and coping better in a stressful situation.

Breathing exercises

Even the lowest level of stress can bring about an increase in your rate of breathing, and long-term or severe stress can disrupt normal breathing rhythms entirely. These kinds of changes in your breathing can upset the normal body chemistry over long periods of time, and can cause many of the symptoms already mentioned, including panic, feeling faint, tingling, and poor concentration. So learning simple ways to restore your normal breathing patterns can be amazingly effective and restorative.

Lifestyle changes

Taking regular breaks, eating healthily, and being more active will all be of advantage. Making sure to get a good night's sleep, and looking at ways to improve work/life balance is part of this too. This may just sound like the kind of health advice you've heard before, many times. But this is different. This kind of change is an extremely powerful one if you want to overcome stress.

Social Support

A trusted friend or family member, or someone going through the same thing can provide amazing support when you are stressed. And most of the organizations offering advice or information will also provide support – a supportive ear, or a shoulder to cry on. All of this helps us to cope so much better. We all need this kind of support. It's a basic human need. And we all benefit from a friendly ear, a guiding hand, or an objective sounding board.

▶ 4 Look at things differently

This last line of attack is all about how we perceive the stressor. We know that differences between people exist in this respect. But it is definitely possible to change your view of life from a 'glass half empty', to a 'glass half full'. This can be a major part of managing stress. Here are some ways of doing this:

Sorting out priorities

It's easy to feel that your life is in a mess and that you can't cope. But coping strategies such as sorting out priorities and becoming more organized can make all the difference.

Thinking habits

The way we habitually see life can encourage or discourage stress. The perpetual negative thinker, or the person who sets standards which are too high for themselves, is actually producing their own stress. Raising awareness of these and other unhelpful thinking habits, and how to make changes to them, can yield great improvements.

Becoming more assertive

This isn't about being aggressive and getting your own way. It's about making sure you're not the doormat, giving in to others all the time and putting yourself last. But it can also be about not dominating and pushing your way through life. What assertiveness is about is mutual respect, listening, compromise, and being able to say what you want or need in a relaxed and warm way. Sounds easy when it's put that way, but there's a bit of a knack to it.

Four lines of attack to beat stress	
IMPROVE UNDERSTANDING	REMOVE THE CAUSE
Have a check-up at the doctor's.	Think it through.
Read all about it.	Take advice if needed.
CUSHION YOURSELF	LOOK AT THINGS DIFFERENTLY
Relaxation	Sort out your priorities
Breathing	Think positively
Breaks	Healthy thinking
Talk to those you trust	Be assertive
Good diet	Be more in the here and now
Enjoyable exercise	Better coping mechanisms
Plenty of sleep	Focus on solutions not problems
Build resilience	Be more positive and smile more

Stress and your 'automatic' nervous system

The body's 'automatic', or to use the correct term 'autonomic', nervous system, has already been introduced. This is the system which looks after the functions of the body which we don't have direct control over ourselves; functions such as breathing, digesting our last meal, or the heart pumping blood around the body. So, the autonomic nervous system, or ANS, underlies all other processes and functions of our body, and is therefore involved in everything we do. How this process operates has been studied for many years.

As long ago as 1908, two researchers, Yerkes and Dodson were looking at how performance on a physical task varied depending on the level of ANS alertness; that is our readiness for action, or 'arousal'. The two researchers found that there was a best or 'optimum' level of arousal for each physical task, and that levels lower or higher than this would reduce performance. They illustrated this with their famous 'arousal curve', which graphs arousal against performance.

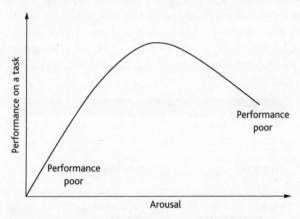

How ANS arousal affects performance on a particular task.

So, what we are looking for is a careful balance. It's all about having the right amount of arousal for the job in hand. But this research and the 'arousal curve' have been misinterpreted by many people.

Mythbuster: Arousal is the same as stress

Many people have assumed wrongly that 'arousal' is the same as 'stress', and have therefore concluded that this early research meant that you had to be stressed by just the right amount to do well on tasks, but less or more than that would reduce performance. This incorrect assumption has led to there being a common idea (or myth) that people do better at work if they are a little stressed, so-called 'good stress' or 'eustress'. This has contributed to increased levels of stress in the workplace over many decades, and is still a widely held belief. *But arousal itself is not stress.* The connection is that if a person appraises a situation as beyond their ability to cope, or places too much importance on the outcome of the task, this is construed by the ANS as a threat and so these thoughts produce *extra* arousal, over the optimum level for that task, and *it's this extra arousal which reduces performance.* As already explained, the extra arousal is there to provide a physical response, has nowhere to expend itself, and is experienced as stress.

THE GOLDILOCKS PRINCIPLE – JUST THE RIGHT AMOUNT OF AROUSAL

You could think of physiological arousal as providing the body with just the right amount of fuel and alertness it needs to put in the required level of effort and muscle tension, for the task in hand.

We require little effort, or muscle tension to watch TV or read a book, so the optimum level of arousal is low. But if we have to dig the garden or play squash, we need much more effort, we need to be much more ready for action, and we also need much more muscle tension.

Take swimming as another example. You need to be fairly physically aroused to be able to swim. The level of physical arousal needed to write an e-mail will be less than this, and the level needed for a difficult rock climb, probably more. Being too 'chilled out' or too 'hyped up' is likely to interfere with performance on all three of these tasks.

Some arousal or 'alertness' of the ANS is needed for every task, even being asleep, when our heart continues to beat, and processes such as breathing, blood circulation, perspiration, digestion, production of urine, continue.

The most favourable level of arousal is greater for physical tasks than for mental tasks. So if you arrive at an exam with arousal more suited to a hill run because of stress, this will be way too high for the very cerebral task of a written exam, and this will mean you'll perform less well.

This effect of there being a clear optimal level of arousal, with performance falling away quickly just above and below this becomes stronger the more complicated the task. This agrees with our experience. Stress can make us stumble over the keyboard, but we can still make a cup of coffee with relative ease.

A 'medium level' of arousal would probably suit most everyday tasks, like walking, cooking, washing the car, or shopping.

This means that when faced with any task, be it digging the garden, vacuuming, having a drink with friends, an appraisal at work, a job interview, or an exam, being too relaxed or too aroused will both mean we won't do as well as we might otherwise have done.

It seems to me that the 'fight or flight' reaction is an example of where the highest level of arousal is actually the optimum required for the very physical task in hand. In other words we need maximum arousal to either fight or run away.

Consequences of stress for our health*

We've already seen that stress is a normal human response, like feeling hungry or thirsty. And as such it is harmless. But just like thirst or hunger, if it is too extreme or goes on too long, there will be implications for health. Some people are better at managing stress than others, but *everyone* has a point beyond which they cannot continue to manage it without it leaving its mark. This may be physical, psychological or behavioural, but it will have an effect on overall health and wellbeing.

The longer the stress continues, the more serious the effects can become. You may become exhausted, chronically agitated and unable to sleep. This can sometimes lead to a complete inability to cope and withdrawal from the day-to-day routine, or to a state of anxiety, or clinical depression. There is evidence to suggest that stress may play a part in causing a number of common physical and psychological symptoms and conditions such as:

▶ heart disease

▶ high blood pressure

▶ insomnia

▶ muscle pains

▶ irritable bowel syndrome

▶ chronic fatigue

▶ panic disorder

▶ phobias

▶ OCD

▶ anxiety

▶ depression.

Additional physical conditions, which can be made worse by stress, include asthma, migraine, indigestion, psoriasis, eczema, and others. Stress can also compromise the immune system, making you more likely to catch the viruses which are going around, such as colds, flu and stomach upsets.

There's no doubt that if you can manage your stress better, not only will you feel better for it, but your general health and wellbeing are going to improve too, making you more resilient to stress in the first place. It's a 'win-win' situation for sure. There will be more on how to build resilience to stress in Chapter 3.

SIGNS YOU SHOULD SEE THE DOCTOR

The majority of stressed people can manage to deal with this without the help of their doctor. But for some people, it can all be too much, especially if it goes on for a long time, or there are multiple stressors, or there are underlying health issues. But when is it time to see your doctor? It's time if you feel it's time, but also if you can tick any one of these:

▶ experiencing marked distress

▶ can't cope with work or everyday life

▶ sudden change in usual personality or behaviour

▶ suicidal thoughts or plans

▶ self-harming

▶ feeling very low or depressed

▶ feeling very anxious

▶ frequent panic attacks or panic feelings

▶ can't sleep

▶ can't eat

▶ lashing out physically or verbally

- withdrawing from everyday life

- hurting those you love

- in a 'daze'

- having flashbacks

- hallucinations (seeing or hearing what's not there)

- feeling everyone is against you

- physical symptoms which concern you

- if a loved one or close friend says they think you should.

Try it now

Stillness

1 Read what to do first, then try it with your eyes closed.
2 Find somewhere comfortable where you can sit down for five minutes.
3 Sit down, uncross your legs, and have your arms comfortably by your side.
4 Begin to bring your thoughts to yourself, just sitting there.
5 Close your eyes gently (optional), and become aware of your breathing. Take a gentle breath in, and in your own time, sigh it back out, allowing your shoulders to relax.
6 Now in your own time, as you breathe in slowly, silently place the word 'SO' on your inward breath, and as you breathe out gently, place the word 'STILL' on your outward breath.

Repeat step six for 1–2 minutes (or longer if you have time).

When is stress an illness?

Neither the World Health Organization (WHO) classification, nor the American Psychiatric Association's Diagnostic Criteria, which are the gold standards in classifying physical and psychological illnesses have a listing for what we might call 'everyday stress'. That's the kind of stress we have talked about so far in this book, and which most of us are familiar with. As we have already seen, this kind of stress is not, in itself, an illness or a disease, though in some circumstances it can contribute to ill health.

But these listings do include as medical disorders three stress-related conditions. Although the definitions from each organization vary slightly, here is a general summary of how these are described (but these definitions don't apply if a person is bereaved).

Condition	Criteria for diagnosis	Duration
Acute stress reaction or disorder	An immediate reaction to an exceptional physical or mental stressor, such as an accident, an assault, being sacked or a domestic fire. Characterized by an initial state of 'daze', followed by a changing picture of anxiety, anger, despair, over activity or withdrawal. Appears within minutes of the stressor's impact, but the symptoms are much reduced within two to three days.	No more than four weeks
Adjustment disorder	This can begin up to three months after an identifiable stressor. Characterised by marked distress which is over and above what would be expected, and causes significant impairment in the person's social life and/or work or study.	No more than six months after stressor has gone.
Post-traumatic stress disorder (PTSD)	Caused by a traumatic event which would cause distress in practically anyone. Characterized by recurrent nightmares, flashbacks, hallucinations, intense reaction to similar events, avoidance of links to the trauma, and general inability to cope with everyday life.	In excess of four weeks.

In all three of these cases, the person involved should seek medical help. This may well happen anyway as a matter of course, because of the distress they are experiencing. These conditions will usually require treatment from a psychiatrist or clinical psychologist, and are dealt with differently from general everyday stress.

PTSD has come very much into the public eye in recent years, in the wake of recent air, sea, fire and other disasters. Veterans of Vietnam, the Falklands, Iraq, Afghanistan and other conflicts also suffer from its effects in considerable numbers. PTSD has been found to be brought on not only by war and major disasters, but from such incidents as robbery, rape, sexual or physical abuse, violent crime, or serious accidents. Even jurors in particularly traumatic court cases can be affected.

Try it now

Relax your mouth and eyes

You may be surprised to discover that when we are thinking, our eyes, mouth and tongue make very tiny movements which we are not aware of. They are tiny, but they will be there. So take a few moments, and focus on allowing your eyes, mouth, lips and tongue to just relax and stay still. Let any tension go from round your eyes and mouth, or from your tongue. Eyes, mouth, lips, tongue, all still, all completely relaxed.

WHAT ABOUT MEDICATION?

Doctors will often prescribe medication for their patients if they are stressed, and this is just another form of cushioning, and can be an effective one, especially in the short-term. Prescribed medication like this has its place in the treatment of stress. If you see your doctor, it is one of a number of options that will be considered (see below) to best meet your needs. Some doctors do treat stress themselves, using a combination of medication and advice based on experience acquired during years of practice.

Remember this

Whether or not you are currently taking medication for stress, if you have any questions about it, your doctor is the person to address these to. Likewise you shouldn't reduce or alter your dosage without talking this over with your doctor.

▶ SSRIs

Most people have heard of a drug called Prozac (fluoxetine). Prozac is an antidepressant, one of the first of a class of drugs known as selective serotonin reuptake inhibitors (SSRIs) which alter the way the brain chemistry works, so that the levels of serotonin are increased. It was soon realized that many of these drugs also reduce anxiety, so SSRIs are commonly prescribed for anxiety and depression, both of which are common outcomes of stress. Like all drugs, they have potential side effects but if properly used together with appropriate advice they can be of great benefit. Though these medications begin to act straight away, it can take ten days or more to actually begin to feel the benefits, and perhaps another week or two to gain maximum benefit. So, it's important to bear with it, and things will improve.

▶ Valium

Valium is a very well-known and effective tranquillizer, which reduces tension and anxiety, but it should only ever be used in the short term because it becomes habit forming, after only a short time. However, it can be a life-line in certain circumstances, perhaps for a close family member's funeral, or to tide a very stressed and anxious person over until longer term medication, or other stress management techniques begin to have an effect.

▶ Beta blockers

One of the most useful drugs for what is known as performance stress (for example, for driving tests, or speaking in public) is a non-sedating drug called a beta blocker, a drug which blocks the 'beta' or cardiac effects of adrenalin, the stress hormone. It will slow and regulate the heart and stop palpitations, inducing a feeling of calmness. Beta blockers also help to reduce shaking and tremor, so are useful for musicians or magicians who are nervous during performances. The names of most beta blockers end with 'olol', for example, propranolol. They usually can't be used for those with asthma, but for others they can be very useful.

▶ Symptomatic relief

Other medications can be used to give symptomatic relief for the problems produced or aggravated by stress. So you might be prescribed medication for diarrhoea, or for irritable bowel syndrome, or for eczema which has worsened. Pain relief can be given for the pain brought on by tense muscles.

Drug name(s)	Main effect(s)
Valium	Tranquillizer
Fluoxetene (Prozac)	SSRI
Citalopram (Cipramil)	SSRI
Paroxetine (Seroxat)	SSRI
Sertraline (Lustral)	SSRI
Propranolol	Beta blocker
Atenolol	Beta blocker
Paracetemol	Relief of stress-induced symptoms

Types of medication

Other approaches to managing stress

People who are experiencing stress say over and over that what they need is someone to listen to their story, and clear advice on what to do to get better. They want to be able to manage it themselves, particularly in the long term, and many would rather not use medication. Cognitive behaviour therapy (CBT) has proved itself in numerous research studies to be an extremely effective therapy of this kind. The majority of techniques you are learning in this book are based on this therapy. Later in the book, you'll also find successful techniques based on two other very effective schools of thought: mindfulness in Chapter 9, and neurolinguistic programming (NLP) in Chapter 10. Each of these mindsets, when applied to stress, offers powerful tools which can increase understanding, and allow you to make changes to the way you think, feel and behave.

Remember this

CBT combines two very effective forms of therapy: cognitive therapy and behaviour therapy.

Cognitive therapy works from the viewpoint that certain ways of thinking can be causing and maintaining symptoms, such as stress or anxiety. This kind of thinking has been called 'distorted thinking'. Challenging and changing these distorted thoughts can lessen stress and anxiety.

Behaviour therapy aims to weaken the connection which has grown between situations and unhelpful reactions to them, like stress or anxiety.

MAIN FEATURES OF COGNITIVE BEHAVIOUR THERAPY

Changing thoughts, feelings and behaviour lies at the heart of CBT, and this can be applied to numerous aspects of human experience, not just stress. There are a number of core aspects to CBT, and although there is no 'therapist' actually present with you as you are reading this book, you'll find these are being used to help you deal with your stress all through the book.

Although CBT is known as a 'talking therapy', this is to distinguish it from the more practical therapies such as aromatherapy or medication. It isn't 'just talking'. It's talking (or in this case, reading) with a carefully chosen and planned purpose and direction.

CBT is based on the idea that it is our internal *thoughts* which bring about our feelings and behaviours, not external things, like people, situations and events. The strength of this idea is that we can change the way we think – so we can change how we feel and behave for the better – even if the situation itself does not change, or can't be changed. The goal of therapy is to learn new ways of reacting and behaving.

CBT is teamwork. The therapist's role is to listen, teach and encourage. Specific techniques/concepts are taught during each session.

Therapists ask questions, and encourage you to ask questions such as, 'How do I really know that those people are talking about me?' 'Could they be talking about something else entirely?'

Between therapy sessions, you will be reading small amounts of user friendly material, completing questionnaires, or diaries, or practising techniques just learned. Just as in this book.

CBT is *non-directive* in the sense that it doesn't tell you how you should feel, or what your goals should be. It is *directive* in the sense that you are shown how to think and behave, in ways which will help you reach your goals.

Who can help you with your stress?

There are many sources of advice about how to manage your stress. Reading this book and following its advice is one option, and self-help of this kind has worked for many thousands of people. But this might not suit everyone, or it may not be enough. What else is available in the way of treatment, advice or support? Each local area has many alternative and complementary therapies, and these will be explored in Chapter 11. Chapter 13 will look at user friendly ways technology or the internet can help beat stress. For now, what's out there in terms of health professionals, or other support?

YOUR DOCTOR

Your doctor is often the first port of call if you are suffering from stress, just as it is if you have a medical problem. You probably feel unwell, and have physical symptoms, so it makes sense. Doctors see stressed people literally every day, but as in most professions, some have more expertise in this area than others. Don't be afraid to try another member of the practice to compare what's available to you. Understanding stress and dealing with it isn't easy for the doctor or the patient.

The doctor may treat you herself, or give you booklets to read. Some practices have a specialist computer system or a specially trained nurse or Stress Adviser for you to work with over a number of visits. You may be offered medication. Some doctors will refer you on to specialist advice or support, including CBT, either within the practice or elsewhere. This may be with a stress counsellor, clinical psychologist, community psychiatric nurse (CPN), or other professional, depending on where you live. It's unlikely you would be referred to a psychiatrist, as they mainly treat mental illnesses such as schizophrenia or bipolar disorder.

OCCUPATIONAL HEALTH AND WELFARE SERVICES

Staff in Occupational Health and Welfare Departments in the workplace are trained to address the problems created by workplace stress (WRS), as well as stress caused at home or elsewhere. They will treat your case as confidential. Your workplace may have an Employee Assistance Programme offering free and confidential advice off-site for a wide range of problems including stress and bullying.

THE CLINICAL PSYCHOLOGIST

Clinical psychologists have a first degree in psychology, and two or three years' postgraduate study covering all of the clinical applications of psychology, including adult mental health, physical and mental disability. Most psychologists will use a range of behavioural and cognitive techniques, including CBT for stressed or anxious patients. People suffering from phobias, panic disorder, PTSD, adjustment disorders, acute stress reaction, and OCD are also treated by clinical psychologists.

NURSE PRACTITIONERS

Specially trained nurses, such as nurse practitioners, or nurse therapists, are often attached to a doctor's practice, or to psychology or other departments in the NHS, or in private health care. They can assess your needs, and take you through a stress management programme over a number of sessions.

COMMUNITY PSYCHIATRIC NURSES

Psychological services may differ from area to area and from country to country. Many GPs now have direct access to Community Psychiatric Nurses (CPNs) who work in the community as a team, and can usually advise you about managing stress.

COUNSELLORS AND THERAPISTS

Here are some guidelines if you are looking for a counsellor or therapist, whether locally or on-line:

▶ Most types of counselling are not 'advice-giving', and the stressed person who is essentially well both medically and mentally, needs clear practical advice on how to manage stress, the kind this book contains. So counselling in its pure non-advice-giving sense is unlikely to be a preferred option for dealing with stress. However, the term 'counsellor' can be used in many ways, and some counsellors will be able to help you with stress.

- Make sure you know what is being offered by the counsellor or therapist before you commit. To be effective, this should be similar to what you see in this book.

- Anyone can call themselves a counsellor or therapist at the present time, so never just answer an advert in a paper or on the internet. Ask for a recommendation from someone you know who has been successfully helped with stress. Alternatively, ask for the name of a satisfied customer, who wouldn't mind you talking to them.

- Choose someone who works for a reputable organization.

- Only go to see a private counsellor or therapist whose methods are clearly explained and acceptable, who has appropriate insurance, and whose qualifications are accredited by a recognized authority.

As part of the journey towards managing stress, non-directive counselling can help, in addition to clear-cut stress advice, because talking over your experiences in a safe place can be very helpful, and counsellors do this extremely well. An objective sounding board can also help to clarify the source of stress, and talk through options for reducing or removing it.

Remember this

Don't try to make too many changes or try too many new ideas all at the same time. This just adds to your stress. One or two at a time is fine, then try some others when these are established.

VOLUNTARY GROUPS OR CHARITIES

In many areas of the UK you will have access to advice about managing stress, through local voluntary groups, charities or advice centres, most of which provide sound advice along with important support. Provision does tend to be patchy across the country though. Online there are numerous support groups and discussion groups. As usual, it is advisable to check that what is being provided by such organizations is sound before seeking their help. These do suit some people, but others do not like this method and prefer a one-to-one approach with more privacy.

SELF-HELP/BIBLIOTHERAPY

Many people will not even need the support of such groups, and once aware of their problem they will be able to help themselves simply by gaining access to appropriate books, CDs or DVDs, either by buying them or borrowing them from the local library. There are lots of these resources around, and most are very helpful. Some libraries now have a special 'Bibliotherapy' area, with specialist books and leaflets on many aspects of health, and sometimes they also offer group or one-to-one sessions. Some GPs will now refer you to your local library for 'Bibliotherapy'.

LOCAL ADVICE OR COURSES IN STRESS MANAGEMENT

Again provision is patchy, but there are well organized stress management courses or relaxation groups run by adult or community education or their equivalent, or by health promotion or other statutory services. Many universities and colleges also now engage in outreach work which includes courses in stress management and assertiveness based in local communities. Advice centres, community projects specifically aimed at improving general or mental health, and women's centres are all likely to be able to offer help too, sometimes on a one-to-one basis. Again, it is useful to check out what exactly is being provided at such a centre, as this can vary substantially. Information about these is usually easy to find, as they advertise widely and will have an internet presence, or may well drop leaflets off at local libraries or GP surgeries.

Focus points

1. Managing stress is best done using four lines of attack: increase your knowledge and understanding, resolve the cause, cushion yourself, and change how you look at the situation.
2. Stress is not an illness itself, but it can make certain illnesses and conditions worse, and play a role in causing others.
3. Stress management techniques are effective and well researched: stress management programmes or advice based on cognitive behaviour therapy (CBT) are very effective when dealing with stress. Aspects of mindfulness and NLP (neurolinguistic programming) can also be of benefit to many people.
4. The doctor can prescribe a range of useful medication if self-help isn't enough.
5. A range of health professionals and other services can also provide effective stress management advice.

3

How to be more resilient

Resilience is all about your ability to withstand stress. In this chapter, you'll find out how vulnerable you are to stress, and learn how to build your resilience so you are better able to cope with it.

What is resilience?

We probably all know someone who is particularly liable to feeling stressed. A relative, friend or neighbour we expect to become nervous and excitable for what we may see as the smallest reason. And we all know someone who isn't – someone who is solid as a rock and everyone can rely on to cope with anything, no matter what. Many people remember how Princess Diana, before her death in a tragic car accident in 1997, was said to have called her butler, Paul Burrell, 'her rock'.

Building up your resilience is about making sure you are more like the second person, the rock, rather than the first. But aiming to be *more* like the second is enough. Not everyone can actually be the stress-free rock. Even the stress-free rock will have their tipping point, and will feel stress too, if things get too much, even for them. Many will also remember some years later, seeing Paul Burrell on the reality show 'I'm a Celebrity, Get me out of Here', in a complete state of panic when faced with one of the physical challenges on the show, which happened to press his particular stress button. No one is immune to stress. We all have our 'stress buttons' which can be pressed to bring about stress.

How do you feel?

Here are five key ideas from this chapter to think about now. They will be discussed later:

1 Compared to the people you know, how vulnerable to stress would you say you are?

   a   Much less

   b   A bit less

   c   About the same

   d   A bit more

   e   Much more

   f   Don't know

   g   Not sure

2 Why do you think that is? Is it your (choose all that apply):

   a Personality

   b Job

   c Previous experiences

   d Not having a job

   e Just chance

   f Your current life situation

   g Your genes

   h Coping strategies

   i Your mindset

   j Don't know

   k None of these

   l Other

3 Roughly how stressful would you rate your current day-to-day life to be? Rate this on a scale of 0, being no stress at all, to 100, being as stressed as you can possibly imagine.

4 How much time on average do you spend doing things which are likely to counteract stress:

   a Every day?

   b Every week?

5 How many people can you talk to that you trust, and who will be supportive and not judge you?

   a None

   b One

   c One to five

   d More than five

   e Don't know

   f Not sure

The 'Stress Equation' – you plus what equals stress?

Professor Cary Cooper has written and researched extensively on stress, and developed what he calls a 'stress equation' to describe how stress affects us. Professor Cooper recognized that some people react more to stress than others. His equation shows how stress from whatever source simply joins together and results in symptoms and outcomes for each of us. But, as you can see there is an added contribution corresponding to how vulnerable we are to stress in the first place, because of our genes and other factors which we'll explore later in the chapter.

$$\boxed{\text{Life Stress}} + \boxed{\text{Work Stress}} + \boxed{\text{Individual Vulnerability}} = \boxed{\text{Stress Symptoms/Outcomes}}$$

So how stressed we feel on a particular day is the total of life stresses, such as debt or problem teenagers, added to any stress we have at work, such as a new more difficult boss, added to a chunk of stress corresponding to how vulnerable we ourselves are to stress.

VULNERABLE OR RESILIENT?

We don't all react to situations the same way. The same situation doesn't stress us all equally. Take a traffic jam, moving house, a looming deadline at work, or giving a talk. We will all react differently, because we are all different in the following three ways, and each of these will affect your vulnerability to stress:

1 Your basic personality traits. We all know how different these can be. This profoundly affects whether you perceive a situation to be stressful or not.

2 The previous experiences you've had in life, both growing up and as adults. These can pre-dispose us to react in certain ways to events later in life. You may also have learned poor coping skills for dealing with stress that make matters worse.

3 Some people's nervous systems are more 'labile', or in other words, they have a nervous system which is more likely to become aroused in the first place. This is sometimes called being 'highly strung', or 'of a nervous disposition', and is usually something you are born with.

For some of us, these three factors will make us more likely than most to feel stressed. But for others, these factors will operate a protective effect, endowing us with our own protective resilience from stress – these will probably be the natural rocks amongst us. We can't really choose these characteristics, so we all have a basic in-built level of either vulnerability or resilience to stress. Over the whole population, there will be wide variations, forming a continuum or spectrum of resilience. But wherever we fall on this line, it is still going to be possible to make substantial improvements, and move along to a higher resilience level.

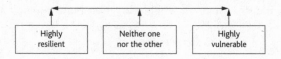

Where do you feel your place on this line would be? In this chapter, I'll explore the main factors which can make a person vulnerable to stress, so that it's easier to understand this better. But I'll also show you ways to improve your resilience, and make some progress towards the left of this line, no matter what your starting point is.

Try it now

Just smile
When you smile, your brain immediately produces special chemicals called endorphins, which make you feel happier. So whenever you can, smile or laugh. This works even if you fake the smile, and don't feel it inside.

WHO IS VULNERABLE TO STRESS?*
Our physical make-up, passed to us in our genes from our parents and grandparents, decrees our hair and eye colour, skin type, sex, and much, much more. Professor Hans Eysenck in 1967 suggested that some of us are born with an autonomic nervous system (ANS) which reacts more easily than others. He suggested that variations in this 'lability' of the ANS produced a range of

possible life experiences for each of us. Very low lability would produce a sense of stability, and you would grow up to be more of the 'rock' mentioned earlier. High lability gives us an experience of emotionality or stress in response to life events, making you grow into the highly strung, nervy people we all know well.

This would mean that for some people, it takes much less to produce a feeling of stress than for others. This is not a sign of weakness as is thought by many people, it is simply a sign of individual biological difference, in the same way that your height or your eye colour can vary. It's in our genes. So a very reactive ANS produces jumpy, anxious people. But a slow to react ANS means a lot of stimulation is needed to create a 'buzz', and this produces people who enjoy bungee jumping and fast cars. Such people appear to thrive on stress, but in reality they are not truly stressed at all.

A labile, fast-acting nervous system would actually have been a positive advantage for our ancestors, because in terms of self-preservation, our distant relative with the labile nervous system would have been able to react to and deal with a dangerous predator far more quickly and effectively. They would have been the survivors in prehistoric life when physical threat was frequent, and may even have been admired greatly for their lightning reaction to danger. It's only in the modern world that it becomes a problem. Being able to react quickly and fight, flee or freeze rapidly and effectively won't help to meet that tight deadline or pay those debts off.

CAN YOU HAVE A VULNERABLE PERSONALITY?

There is no such thing as a stress-proof personality. That would be too easy. Nor is there a particularly stress-inducing personality. It's not about a particular stressor, or a particular personality. It's about the mix of the two, and what this throws up on a particular day, in a particular situation. Let's look at two examples.

In many aspects of life in the UK, if you are a perfectionist, you stand a high chance of being vulnerable to stress. Take the perfectionist working in a job such as social work, teaching, or police work, who may find themselves stressed because they don't have the time or resources to deal with everything perfectly, and as they would like. Their in-tray is never empty. The loose ends are never tied up. On the other hand, all things being equal, the perfectionist working as a pharmacist, accountant, banker or radiologist, where performance must be as complete and mistake-free as possible, is much more likely to be stress free.

Another example would be a person who could be obsessional from time to time. This is not the person with extreme behaviour such as obsessional hand-washing or cleaning. No, many completely ordinary people have an element of obsessional behaviour within their personality which is not a sign of any kind of problem. For example, they may demand high standards for themselves and others in terms of punctuality, conscientiousness or conformity, or be unable to tolerate variations from their chosen way of doing things. Such individuals have very fixed thinking, and are strongly resistant to change and new ideas. So, if their environment does not comply with their particular standards, stress will probably be the outcome.

TYPE A AND TYPE B PERSONALITIES

Another very well-known model linking personality and stress was developed by two cardiologists, Dr Meyer Friedman and Dr Ray Rosenman in 1974. They described two extremes of personality and thinking style known as Type A and Type B. Type A is prone to stress, whereas Type B is less so, and therefore less likely to succumb to stress-related illnesses. Take the two typical examples of behaviour and thinking described in the following case studies.

Case study

Tamara: Typical Type A

Tamara is 34 and manager of a small but growing electronics firm. As soon as her electronic alarm beeps in the morning, she jumps out of bed and into the shower. She snatches a piece of toast and black coffee while at her laptop, finalizing paperwork she was working on last night, then pushes the laptop into its case and heads for the car. The car beeps to alert her to the fact that her service is way overdue, and she mutters angrily to herself about how she never has time to arrange things like car services, and dentist appointments. She has just enough time to get to work to facilitate the first of several important meetings today. If this first meeting goes to plan, this could mean work for everyone for at least a year ahead. Within minutes Tamara hits roadworks and slow-moving traffic, and another car pulls in sharply in front of her. 'Idiot' she snaps, hitting the horn. The tension now in her hands and forearms travels to her shoulders and she can feel her heart rate beginning to rise. 'Traffic', she fumes. 'Why didn't I leave earlier?' She grips the wheel ever more tightly, and increases the volume of the music on the radio. Tamara gets to work late, with no time to prepare for her meeting, and barks at her assistant to get her a coffee, and why hadn't she warned her about the roadworks?

 ## Case study
Gary: Typical Type B

Gary is 37 and manages a small but growing specialist knitwear factory. He wakes to the sound of relaxing music on his radio, and gets up slowly and stretches. Important meeting on today, so he's allowed extra time to get to work in case of traffic. After an energizing shower, he sits down to breakfast and a chat with his wife. He flicks through the paper then walks out to the car, noticing the plants he'd put in at the weekend were doing well. His car has just returned from its regular service and purrs into life. After a few minutes he finds himself in slow-moving traffic, and is surprised at first when the car alongside of him suddenly pulls in before him, but reckons the couple inside must be in a hurry to get somewhere, so he quickly forgets about it. He puts on his favourite radio channel to listen to while in the traffic. On arriving at work, he has time to look over the day's appointments before his assistant arrives.

These are rather stereotypical views of the two extremes, Tamara being a Type A and Gary a Type B. But it's not difficult to see how their different styles of thinking and behaving are affecting their every move. Many people will actually show a mixture of Type A and Type B behaviour, and how you behave can depend on the situation too. So where do you think you fit in? Check out these descriptions:

The following behaviours are typical of the stress-inducing behaviour of Type A:

- does everything quickly – talking, eating, walking
- impatient, inflexible
- overly competitive
- self-imposes deadlines which are too tight
- unable to relax or do nothing without a sense of guilt
- frequently does two or more things at once
- makes no allowance for delays
- becomes oblivious to beauty and things of interest around them
- loud, and prone to hostility and aggression, especially to others of Type A
- uses gestures such as a clenched fist, or banging on the table for emphasis.

The following characteristics are typical of Type B:

- free of Type A characteristics!
- feels no need to impress others with their achievements
- able to relax without feeling guilty
- no sense of time urgency
- aware of surroundings
- no in-built hostility or extreme competitiveness
- slow, calm and attentive
- warm, medium volume voice.

VULNERABILITY THROUGH PREVIOUS EXPERIENCES

Vulnerability to stress is brought about for some people through one or more negative life events in childhood or in adulthood. In 1988, David Barlow described how having experienced uncontrollable or unpredictable life events in the past can make your ANS more reactive. In other words, your ANS can become sensitized to stress, and you may even have some 'hot buttons' or especially sensitive topics or situations which can produce an excessively stressed reaction.

Knowing how to deal effectively with stress does not come naturally. It is during childhood and throughout life when we have to deal with stress, that we develop strategies for coping with it. We acquire these strategies in the main by copying others, or by applying what we think is common sense, or using what we find works.

If our parents reacted to stress by running about wringing their hands, or by bottling it all up, we may well do the same. After all, we learn how to tie our laces and to speak by copying the adults around us, so it's not surprising that we learn how to deal with stress in a similar way. We also learn ways of coping with stress from friends and the wider society. So, if our friends say that taking your mind off things is a useful strategy, we are likely to give it a try, and if it works, this will become part of our repertoire for dealing with stress.

Some of these coping strategies are helpful, some unhelpful. But many people who are finding stress is getting on top of them are likely to start using coping strategies which are at best not helping, and at worst, may even be making matters worse. Learning stress management is about learning a range of strategies which can really help to deal with stress in different situations, and we will look in detail at these all through the book. But it is also useful to be aware of the kinds of unhelpful strategies people might already be using to cope with their stress.

COPING STRATEGIES THAT MAKE MATTERS WORSE

The strategies people who are already stressed tend to go for also tend to be the ones that will make matters worse. So what then happens is that the body will rapidly become tired, drained and less resilient. A vicious circle is formed whereby the individual will feel more stressed and probably become physically and psychologically ill, and still nothing has been done to tackle the original situation. This is probably because their ANS is already aroused by the stress, and this encourages most of the following coping mechanisms, which only increase the problem.

▶ Work longer, harder and faster

Many people are stressed because they have too much to do in too little time, both paid and unpaid. Many businesses and services have 'down-sized' to save on costs, but this has simply piled more work onto the remaining staff. So there's more to do, and less time to do it. An understandable reaction to having too much to do is to work harder and work longer hours, to get everything done, and usually with fewer breaks. People miss lunch, or have lunchtime meetings, work late, don't take their days off to catch up, take work home, miss out on holidays and so on. Many have no option as their job and livelihood, or their family's wellbeing, may depend on getting through the workload. 'Presentism' is becoming a problem at work, rather than 'absenteeism', with employers expecting staff to work longer hours to show commitment to the job.

▶ Increased substance use

Many people drink or smoke to excess, and this is often an outcome of even a low level of stress in their lives. The use of prescription and non-prescription drugs is also a common reaction to stress. Not only is this behaviour counter-productive in terms of stress, but the added risks to health are obvious.

▶ Eating

Many people have learned in childhood to associate feeling relaxed and at ease with eating, and it's easy to see how that can happen. Comfort eating is a common reaction to stress, but brings with it weight gain and health risks.

▶ Overactivity

Another common reaction to stress is to keep very busy with other things, sometimes to excess. Every minute of the day can be filled with work, hobbies, clubs, sport or socializing. This has a very draining effect.

▶ Denial

There are various forms of denial, most of them harmful in most situations. The exception to this is the temporary denial which can exert a protective effect in the case of a serious trauma such as the death of a loved one. Denial is particularly common amongst those who see admitting a problem with stress as a sign of weakness. This is an outcome of a society which values coping and success, and sees an inability to cope as failure.

▶ Escapism

Many people simply escape from whatever situation they are having problems with, rather than dealing with it. They might move from job to job, and from relationship to relationship, never attempting to sort out difficulties. This can place the person in something of a downward spiral, with no permanency in any aspect of life.

▶ Taking it out on other people

This takes the form of either blaming others for everything, or taking out feelings of anger and frustration on them. Loved ones will often be the targets for this type of anger. Apart from relieving some of these pent-up emotions, little benefit is achieved by this, and much damage can be done to relationships.

Try it now

Four by four breathing

1 Quietly exhale any breath in your lungs.
2 Breathe in to your own count of four.
3 Hold for four.
4 Breathe back out to the same count of four.

Repeat 1–4, up to four times.

VULNERABILITY THROUGH CONTROL ISSUES

Suzanne Kobasa has highlighted a sense of being in 'control' as an important factor in resilience (more on this later). It's easy to picture how a stressor is likely to be that much more of a problem if we feel at its mercy, with little we can do to affect it or make it stop.

In 1966, J.B. Rotter was also thinking about control in relation to stress. He introduced the concept of 'locus of control', and thought that people either had an 'external locus of control', or an 'internal locus of control'. The term 'locus' just means 'place' or 'location', so Rotter was talking about where people felt control lay in their lives.

If you have an 'external locus of control', you are going to feel that control of your life comes largely from outside of you, from the circumstances and people that surround you,

Rotter thought that those with an external locus of control were more vulnerable to stress in most situations. Such people tend to hold some or all of the following beliefs – what about you?

► I have little influence or control over my life.

► Fate, luck and chance play a crucial role in my life.

► Success is determined by being in the right place at the right time.

► What happens to us is pre-destined.

► Our lives are mainly determined by forces which we cannot control.

► I just have to put up with it, because there's nothing I can do about it.

On the other hand, if you have an 'internal locus of control', you will feel you have your own, internal control over what happens to you, and that your own actions and decisions can actually have an effect on your life.

Sometimes, all that's needed to move your locus of control from outside of yourself, to within your own heart and mind, is to become aware of it.

Remember this

In order to be more resilient, it is better to have an internal locus of control, in other words, to feel you can influence your life, and that it's not all down to chance. So if your locus of control lies outside of you, bring it in to your hands now.

Developing your resilience

In 1979, Suzanne Kobasa, developed her theory of 'hardiness' with respect to the ability of an individual to withstand stress. This is a very similar concept to 'resilience'. After studying a group of executives she suggested that if a person has the three Cs, that is commitment, control and challenge in their lives, they have what she defined as a 'hardy' personality.

I've used the word cushioning, as explained in Chapter 2, as a stress management strategy which lessens the impact of an existing stress, and helps you to be more of a 'rock'. Resilience takes this further in that it's about thinking ahead so that you are already cushioned, and less vulnerable to stress if it comes along. It's a bit like the story of the Three Little Pigs, when the third pig, having had two failed run-ins with the wolf, has his house built of strong brick, rather than straw or sticks to withstand the next attack from the wolf. The moral of this story has been a strong one in Western culture for 200 years or more.

The remainder of this chapter will look at some of the main ways you can go about developing your own resilience to stress.

RESILIENCE AND SOCIAL SUPPORT

There is a bank of evidence to suggest that being part of a social network can provide resilience, and offer protection against stressful life events, and against stress-related ill health. This social and emotional support can come from family, friends, work colleagues or the local community; the more varied and extensive the support the better. Those with little support of this kind are vulnerable to stress, and can find coping with the daily hassles and problems of life difficult.

But people living alone are not the only people who might lack social support. Anyone living in a family or a neighbourhood which does not provide this support is also vulnerable. Many people may even live with others, but find that they have negative social support. Examples of this might be living with a partner or a family member who is openly critical and non-supportive, or a friend who keeps telling you that you should 'pull yourself together' or 'get a life'.

All of us need positive social support if stress is a problem for us. This makes stress easier to cope with and cushions its impact for us. In Chapter 2, when thinking about people's attitudes to stress, I asked you to think about those people who might be supportive to you, and how you could best encourage and make use of that support. You might like to look back at that section now to refresh your memory.

Remember this

Having someone who cares about us, and who is interested in what we do, can bring both a relief of existing stress, and also prevent us feeling stressed in the first place. A problem shared really is a problem halved.

FINDING OUT WHO YOU CAN RELY ON

Have another think about everybody you come into contact with, and the community you live in. You'll need a piece of blank paper in your journal, at least A4 size, and some coloured pens or pencils.

Using colours, in any way you like, draw a straight line up and down the middle of the paper. Then draw another across the paper, half way down. This should divide your sheet into four roughly equal boxes. Now draw a circle about 10 cm across with its centre where the two lines cross. Keep the circle blank for now.

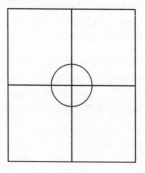

Again, using colours any way you want, write a heading in each box for the four possible sources of support: 'Family and/or partner', 'Friends', 'Organizations' and 'Work'.

If you have a partner are they supportive? If YES, how do they show this to you? Write their name in the appropriate box.

Do you have members of your family who are or could be supportive? If yes, write their names in too.

Now do the same for the remaining three boxes. Fill in the remaining three boxes with any support available to you there.

Are there any other kinds of support you really miss? If so, write these in the centre circle. How could you go about getting this support?

If you already have a good support system, use it to the full, as an outlet for feelings and as a source of encouragement. You should also accept offers of help, and delegate to others to relieve pressure. No need to feel guilty for doing this.

But if your existing support system could do with some building up, or if you're starting at the beginning and trying to build one for yourself, here are some suggestions – note down those you could try:

▶ Take it one step at a time.

▶ Don't forget to look after your existing supportive relationships.

▶ If someone important doesn't understand, if you think it would help, let them read some of this book to help them to understand better, or try explaining it to them yourself.

▶ Create new supportive relationships whenever possible.

▶ Get more involved in your community.

▶ Seek support from an appropriate community organization.

▶ Join a local social club or other group.

- Consult local directories, libraries or advice centres for suitable support, leisure or social facilities. Anything on the internet? There are numerous confidential support and/or counselling groups in every community. Seeking help there isn't a sign of weakness.

- Think about using any support or getting involved in social events which are available at work.

How to use your lifestyle to build resilience

To build and maintain your resilience or 'air bag' of life, there is much more that you can do in terms of your everyday lifestyle. Aim to gradually create a routine for yourself so that the items in the table below will happen every week without you having to plan them. Don't rush at it all at once though. This would be too much for anyone. Take things one or two steps at a time, to fit in with your life. The advice in this book will help you with this.

What to do	How often	Find out more
Talk to someone	Regularly	This chapter
Keep fit	At least twice weekly	Chapter 4
Be active	Every day	Chapter 4
Make time for leisure activities	At least once or twice weekly	Chapter 4
Take breaks	Every day, every week, every few months	Chapter 4
Eat healthily	Every day	Chapter 4
Relax your body	Every day	Chapter 5
Breathe well	Every day	Chapter 5
Calm your mind	Every day	Chapter 6
Think healthily	Every day	Chapter 6
Know your rights, and say what you think.	Every day	Chapter 6

Some ways to use lifestyle to build up your resilience to stress.

Focus points

1. Some people are more likely to feel stressed than others, because of their:

   * very reactive nervous system
   * personality
   * prior experiences
   * poor coping skills
   * lack of social and emotional support
   * feeling of a lack of control
   * lack of confidence.

2. Everyone can improve their resilience to stress. Resilience makes you less vulnerable to stress, and provides a cushion, or buffer, against stressors.

3. If you are vulnerable to stress you can counteract this by developing your resilience.

4. Having some sense of control over your life makes you less vulnerable to stress, and improves resilience.

5. Everyone can learn how to improve their resilience through simple lifestyle changes.

4

How simple lifestyle changes can reduce stress

In Chapter 3 the importance of building resilience to buffer yourself from stress was explained, and different ways to do this were introduced. A key part of this is thinking about your lifestyle, and we have already touched upon some guidelines for lifestyle choices. This chapter will explain this further, and there will be more suggestions on how to make improvements to all aspects of your lifestyle to enhance and strengthen your resilience and ability to cushion yourself from stress.

How do you feel?

Here are five key ideas from this chapter to think about now. They will be discussed later:

1 How would you describe your lifestyle? Don't think too long about this. Choose the four or five words which first come to mind when you think about this. Note these down.

2 Do you get enough time for yourself in the average week?

   a Sometimes

   b Never

   c Every week

3 Do you stop what you're doing, and make time for lunch?

   a Sometimes

   b Never

   c Every day

   d Other

4 Which of the rows (1 to 9) in this table best describes the percentage of your week taken up with work of any kind (paid, voluntary, housework), compared to other parts of your life?

ROW	WORK %	OTHER %
1	100	0
2	90	10
3	80	20
4	60	40
5	50	50
6	40	60
7	20	80
8	0	100
9	Other?	

5 How do you feel about your previous answer?

Work/Life balance

Whatever kind of work we do, whether it is running a company, taking care of children, caring for a disabled relative, volunteering at the local charity shop, or working behind the till at an 'open all hours' shop, it will inevitably shape our life experience as a whole. It will also impact on who we feel we are, and how we feel about ourselves. All this will in turn have a bearing on how we react if some stress comes along.

Remember this

Work/life balance is important even if you are unemployed, or retired, or have poor health or a disability, or just don't need to work to pay the bills. In fact, it's more important, because everyone feels better if they are engaged in meaningful 'work' at least for part of the week. This work doesn't need to be rewarded by money, but it does need to be rewarded with a feeling of having achieved something worthwhile, and meaningful.

HOW IS YOUR WEEK FILLED?

So no matter what your situation in life is, think about how you fill your days.

To help you do this, roughly draw three squares about 8 cm each side on one sheet of paper in your Personal Journal, and place another small square in the bottom right-hand corner (as below). Use colour and artwork if you want! Put a heading at the top of each to represent the three main areas of your life:

1 home, partner and family

2 hobbies and interests

3 work – paid and unpaid.

Jot down a list of the main things you do for each box. Don't go into too much detail, and don't think too hard. You just need a general picture.

So in the home and family section you might put things like washing, ironing, cooking, looking after a pet, decorating, shopping, spending time with your partner, visiting your parents, looking after the kids, and so on.

Under hobbies and interests you could include Sudoku, socializing, sport, music, social networking sites, reading, watching TV, chilling, studying, and so on.

In the work and voluntary work section you might include computer work, talking to people, advising people, selling things, building things and so on.

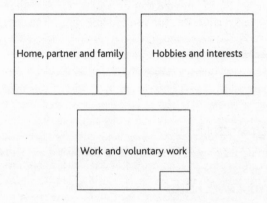

Now go back to your boxes and put a rough estimate of how much time you spend on each item you've listed in an average week. Then add these together and write the total in the corner box.

With the three boxes completed, here are some questions to think about. Note your thoughts on the other side of your sheet of paper.

1 Are you happy with how much time you spend on each item in each box and the overall time spent on each box? If not what might you do about it?

2 How does your week divide up into the three areas? How does that seem to you?

3 And what about time just for you? Me-time. Is there enough? Or is there too much? If not, what can you do about this?

4 Any surprises for you in this activity? Jot down your thoughts.

GETTING THE BALANCE RIGHT

How we spend our time can impact greatly on how we see ourselves, on the health and wellbeing of ourselves and those around us, and on our confidence, life satisfaction, and resilience. Sometimes, the days pass by so quickly that you don't notice that you're not spending enough quality time with family and friends, or with your partner. Or that you're working more and more hours, and missing out on leisure. Or that there is no time in your schedule just for you, no 'me-time'. Then again, you can have too much time on your hands, and be bored and frustrated through not putting all that time to positive use. Becoming a couch potato watching daytime TV every day is an easy habit to slip into, but devastating for your health and your resilience to stress.

CHANGE IS STRESSFUL

A well-known viewpoint about change and stress, and about stressors adding up, was described by Dr Thomas Holmes and Dr Richard Rahe, in their research in 1967. They proposed that the more changes you have been exposed to over the previous 12–24 months, the lower is your current resistance to disease, and the more likely you are to have a physical illness. They developed a 'Life Events Survey' which listed some 43 events, like losing your home or job, going through a divorce, or you or a loved one being ill, with a score assigned to each.

As a general rule, our autonomic arousal is low when our environment is stable and predictable. When we know what to expect, everything is familiar, and there are no surprises. If any change does occur, whether good or bad, we must adapt to that change, and arousal is produced. This means that making too many changes all at the same time is going to create stress for you. So, if you have a choice, spreading out the life changes you want to make over a period of time will be less stressful than making them all at once. I can identify with this point. Before I had learned anything about stress, I graduated from college, moved to a new home, got married, and started an important new job, all within three months. It was only with hindsight that I could explain why the year that followed was something of a high-speed daze.

Lifestyle and stress

A person's lifestyle in terms of their day-to-day activities can either make them more vulnerable to stress or cushion them from it. To find out how, try this short questionnaire. Make a note of your answer to each question.

Do you eat healthily most days?	YES NO
Are you content with how much socializing you are doing?	YES NO
Do you eat breakfast most days?	YES NO
Do you usually take your time when eating meals?	YES NO
Have you clear goals in your life?	YES NO
Do you drink less than three cups of coffee or tea a day?	YES NO
Is your weight in the 'normal' range?	YES NO
Do you almost always have time for tea/coffee breaks?	YES NO
Do you almost always have time for lunch?	YES NO
Is your alcohol intake within recommended levels?	YES NO
Do you have week-long breaks at least twice a year?	YES NO
Do you take exercise most weeks?	YES NO
Are you content with how much is going on in your life?	YES NO
Do you feel you regularly have someone to talk to and share things with?	YES NO
Do you set aside time just to relax most weeks?	YES NO
Is there mostly enough time to do everything you want to do?	YES NO
Do you take part regularly in a leisure pursuit or hobby?	YES NO
Is there enough time just for you in your life?	YES NO
Do you feel you usually get enough sleep?	YES NO

I'm sure you will have gathered by now, that for maximum cushioning from stress in our day-to-day lives, a YES answer for each answer would be preferable. However, we do live in the real world, so most people will circle NO at least a few times, with others ranging upwards from there. The essential point is that the more times NO is chosen in questionnaires of this kind the less an individual is cushioned from stress, and the more likely it is that they may have difficulties coping with stress should it arise. Indeed, a large number of NO answers may be a cause of stress in itself. For example, rushing meals, not taking breaks and not getting enough sleep will make life more stressful.

HOW LIFESTYLE CAN PROVIDE A BUFFER FROM STRESS

This last short and very basic questionnaire, and the previous activity, may have given you a deeper insight into your own lifestyle, or simply confirmed what you knew already. But it's hard to argue against the idea that to manage stress, and maximize resilience, it's vital to look fairly closely at lifestyle in terms of:

▶ how and when we eat and drink

▶ exercise and general activity levels

▶ leisure time

▶ sleep

▶ time to relax

▶ me-time

▶ work/life balance

▶ time management.

This chapter will give you a chance to think about each of these aspects of your lifestyle (though relaxation will be covered in more detail in Chapters 5 and 6), and provide you with many options and choices which could make your lifestyle a more efficient stress buffer, as well as just generally encouraging health, wellbeing and contentment.

Keeping your Personal Journal

Although there will be lots of suggested lifestyle changes, making one or two of these at a time is definitely the best way to go, and the most likely to succeed long-term. No matter how keen and determined you are, attempting too many changes at once is not only likely to fail for practical and motivational reasons, but can produce further stress, since change itself is stressful. Fitting in a game of golf, making time for breakfast every day and cutting down on coffee, can seem easy and a novelty for one week, or even two, but then life can quickly get in the way and the new-found lifestyle can quickly slip away.

But finding half an hour to kick a ball about with the family or the neighbours' kids a couple of times a week to begin with, can be both enjoyable and easy to sustain in the long-term. Further changes can then be built on this firm foundation, over a period of time.

Try it now

Personal Journal

I suggested earlier that having some kind of personal journal to hand when you're reading this book will help you to get more out of the whole process. It's also a good idea to use your journal to keep track of your lifestyle changes, and to keep a simple progress diary. Whatever you've been using so far, for your notes, you could also consider using your mobile phone, or iPad, or making an audio or video recording. Include art work or graphics, if you like. If you're using paper and pen, 'sticky notes' are a good addition, as it's easier to move these around, and that will be a bonus later on. Make your notes short or long, serious or humorous, simple or detailed. It's entirely your call. And it needn't take any time at all to do. Here's what to include:

✳ Give yourself a score each day for how stressed you've felt. Score this out of 10, 0 being not stressed at all, 10 being as stressed as you could possibly imagine. It's easy to forget the 'good days', and this can also draw attention to any patterns or correlations which are going on. You never know what you might discover.

✳ Make a note of how the day has gone, or do this weekly if you prefer. A phrase, a sentence or two, or write as much as you want if you have the time and inclination.

✳ Keep three lists on three separate pages: changes and techniques you're starting *now*, changes and techniques you want to start *soon*, changes and techniques which you'll get to *later*. Including a page reference will make these easier to find later on. Using 'sticky notes' for each item makes it easier to move these around as they move from *soon* to *now*.

Simple changes can give huge benefits

Now it's time to concentrate on those main strategies for stress management which are associated with our everyday lifestyle. This chapter will look at the other key changes which will definitely improve the cushioning effect of your lifestyle and build resilience. Optimizing lifestyle will therefore form an important and long-term part of any personal stress management programme. Some changes are simpler than others. But many have a much larger effect than you might expect. For example, numerous people have noticed a huge improvement just by cutting out caffeine, or eating breakfast for the first time, or by simply having a regular lunchtime walk.

Tick, highlight or make a note of any of the following ideas you think would help you in your life.

Eating and drinking:

▶ Make time to relax and enjoy your meals.

▶ Eat a healthy well-balanced diet, low in sugar, salt and fat, and high in fibre.

▶ Have a good breakfast, don't skip lunch, and avoid sugary snacks or long gaps (two–three hours at most) without eating – this ensures a constant blood sugar level which helps to protect you from stress. Five smaller healthy meals can work better than three big meals, and is certainly better than two big meals and no breakfast.

▶ Avoid too much coffee, tea, chocolate or other food and drinks containing caffeine (e.g. cola, high energy drinks, 'extra' type flu and pain relief). Caffeine produces a feeling of irritability and nervousness. If your body is used to a lot of caffeine, reduce this gradually.

▶ Never use alcohol, tobacco or non-prescription drugs to alleviate stress. Stay within the recommended healthy limits.

Taking breaks:

▶ If you feel pressurized in a situation at work or home, don't make the mistake of working through lunch and tea breaks, and staying late to catch up. That's OK if it's a one-off crisis. But if this happens often, it becomes counterproductive. Who would you rather assessed your blood test, or repaired your filling? Someone who had stopped for their morning tea break, and their lunch break, or someone who had been working for seven hours without a break?

▶ You will be more efficient, get more done and feel better if you take regular breaks. No matter how busy you are, a break will refresh you, allow you to unwind and put things into perspective. And then allow you to carry on more efficiently and less stressed when you get back.

▶ Taking regular breaks allows arousal to be reduced every so often during your day, and will gradually heal your sensitized nervous system. It also means you can maintain an even blood sugar level.

▶ This principle operates at several levels. A ten-minute break every morning, time away from the desk to eat lunch, an afternoon out at the weekend, or two weeks on holiday in the summer all help to inhibit stress all year round, maintain health and build your resilience.

▶ If your life revolves around the needs of others most of the time, make sure that you take some time for yourself, and to be yourself. It really is OK to take time for yourself!

HOW TO MANAGE TIME BETTER

There is no denying that many people have very high workloads, and it seems as if there just aren't enough hours in the day. This is undeniably difficult to deal with, but it is fairly straightforward to organize your time at least a little, and hopefully a lot, better.

Organize your day taking into account when you have most energy. So make plans, compile reports, paint the hall, facilitate meetings, learn about new processes, when you are at your best. And work on routine stuff like e-mails, straightforward phone calls, and form-filling, when your energy and motivation are lower.

Don't check and answer e-mails and voicemail all day; check and answer at the same time once or twice a day. The only reason to do this more often is if your job really demands it, or if you're waiting for an urgent response.

Rather than interrupting what you're doing, make and return routine phone calls in groups at a time you're likely to catch people in.

Use some high energy time to select, plan and prioritize the weeks and months ahead. Set time aside each week to do this. Plan your days, weeks and months. Allocate a reasonable time to complete a piece of work, and stick to it. Know when your targets and deadlines are. Even if you're very busy, it feels much better knowing where you are. Yes, all this may sound nerdy, but if it stops you from being stressed, it can't be all that nerdy, can it?

Don't try to do everything perfectly. Just do what's necessary to complete the task, and tick the boxes. Compare you taking a weekend to paint your 30-foot long, four-feet high plain brick garden wall in a deep rust, to Michelangelo spending four years painting the ceiling of the Sistine Chapel in the Vatican. Both will be fit for purpose. See the difference?

If you have a plan, it's easier to ask for help in advance if you know you're going to need it somewhere down the line. Or to re-arrange minor commitments to suit major ones. Or to say, 'sorry, I just can't fit that in until..., because I have...to do'...if asked to do another task.

Many people become overloaded through saying 'yes' to everything, because they have no clear plan to support them. Indeed, they often don't even know whether they have the time or not, until it's too late. It's even far easier to justify requesting some extra time or help from other members of staff, if you can clearly show why this is needed.

Keep lists of jobs to be done. Divide these into urgent, and non-urgent, and 'only if I have time'. Tick or score these off as you do them – this feels really good, and you can see progress as well as where you are. You can have sticky notes on a poster on the wall, or if you work in a team, have a roll of brown paper along the wall with all the team members' sticky notes together, and easy to move around.

Keep a diary, either hard copy or on your laptop or phone, but somewhere.

Learn to delegate jobs to other people.

Do one job at a time, not three or four! Multi-tasking only works on combinations of activities which are very familiar, and after lots of practice. That's probably why women seem to do this better than men, because they've had so much practice at juggling numerous activities at the same time. For anything new or complicated, or if you need to be creative, or forward thinking, stick to one thing at a time.

Protect time when you need to. Don't answer calls, look at e-mails or respond to interruptions. Unless it's a priority, just explain you're busy right now, but you'll get back to them later. But make sure you do.

Be organized – know where everything is.

LEISURE

Enjoying some sort of leisure activity regularly, and having other interests and pastimes, all act as very effective cushioning against stress.

Leisure pursuits can also provide support through the friendships they can bring, reduce stress by giving you a break, give you something to do if you have too much time on your hands, or provide a new challenge if you need one.

Leisure pursuits help to prevent an individual's identity and self-image relying entirely on the stressful situation, be that at work or home.

Be active – be less stressed

As we all know, regular exercise is very good for your health, but being physically active also has an excellent cushioning effect on stress, and builds resilience. The key is to choose the right kind of exercise for you, and to do it often. The right kind of exercise is the kind you really enjoy doing, and which fits in with your lifestyle. Some forms of exercise bring with them socializing, and some require music, both of which are also good for managing stress. Even if you are initially reluctant, the feel-good factor begins very quickly after you get there and get started, so it's really worth making the effort. One of my coaching clients still has to push himself really hard to get up out of bed, then into the shorts and top, and into the garage to out on the bike ride which makes him feel just great every Sunday morning.

Here are just a few other examples to think about:

Gardening	Pilates
Walking	Belly dancing
Running	Curling
Cycling	Golf
Go to the gym	Ballroom dancing
Yoga	Salsa
Zumba	Rowing
Aerobics	Netball
Ice hockey	Basketball
Bowls	Power walking
Wind surfing	Ice skating
Swimming	Hill running
Tap dancing	Scottish country dancing
Hill walking	Weight training
Five-a-side football	Circuit training
Irish dancing	Football
Squash	Tennis
DVD at home	T'ai Chi

Always check with your doctor if you're unsure about your fitness to begin or resume any exercise or activity routine – though walking is generally OK for most people, and there is usually something to suit every ability. It's best to sign up for a course or join a club if you're new to exercise, so that you build up carefully, and make sure to do some stretches before and after exercise. It's so easy to cause an injury if you don't know what you're doing.

If you choose an activity you enjoy, and proceed carefully, the benefits of regular exercise are truly enormous:

▶ Exercise of whatever kind has the effect of releasing endorphins in the brain. These are chemicals which make you feel good, and enhance your sense of wellbeing. Some people talk about the 'buzz' it gives them, or a 'natural high', and this is real.

▶ More alpha waves are produced, clearing your mind and producing an enjoyable relaxed alertness.

- Some forms of exercise use up feelings of anger and frustration safely. Contact sports such as judo or kick boxing are typical examples of ways to burn off those feelings and their related body chemicals in a safe way.

- Helps to remove unwanted muscle tension, and allows the body to function in its natural way.

- Combats the 'tired all the time' (TATT) fatigue caused by stress.

- Helps you to sleep better.

- Provides a natural way to expend the stress chemicals your body is producing.

- Improves blood flow to the whole body, refreshing and energizing.

- Improves overall health, wellbeing and resilience.

MAKE YOUR DAYS MORE ACTIVE

You can increase your physical activity easily every day, even while you're at work or looking after children or other adults by:

- Taking the stairs rather than the lift – or at least walk up one or two flights if you're in a tall building (except if you have a pram or wheelchair).

- If you have children (or even a dog!), it's easy – kick a ball about, throw a frisbee, take them for a walk, skim stones along the water, build a sandcastle, push them on a swing, and all the rest. So easy to do, and fun. And your kids (or dog) and your relationship with them will benefit too. You may feel too tired after work, but after a bit of a quick rest, getting active can shake that away for you too.

- If you have time, walk round to see a colleague at the other end of the building, rather than e-mailing or phoning.

- Park a bit further away than you need to, and walk the extra distance.

- Volunteer if someone is looking for help which requires activity – tidying a cupboard, moving equipment, youth group leader, planting bulbs, tidying up a local area, whatever.

▶ The old 'get off the bus a stop early' idea is still a good one.

▶ There's always a cleaning or tidying job you can do at home or if you have a garden – vacuuming, cleaning windows, dusting, tidying, brushing up leaves, trimming the hedge. If you live in a flat, what about getting an allotment? Put on some of your favourite fairly fast music to help you along. Use your iPlayer if you're outside. These tasks will all burn calories, and actually make you feel better as you're doing them, with all the benefits already listed. And your home and garden will look better too, which also makes you feel better!

SLEEP

Getting enough sleep is vitally important to refresh both body and brain. If you find getting off to sleep difficult, make sure you take regular exercise (see above) as this will help you sleep. But don't exercise within three hours of bedtime. Also, any form of relaxation or breathing exercise will help you get off to sleep or fall back to sleep if you wake up during the night. This will also ensure that your sleep will be will much more refreshing and reviving. Chapter 6 will explain how to calm an over-active mind and give lots more tips on how to sleep better.

Focus points

1. Changes of any kind in our lives, whether large or small, can be stressful.
2. Getting a good work/life balance is a key part of managing stress.
3. Exercise has many benefits, and helping you cope better with stress is a really important one. It's also great fun, if you take part in exercise you enjoy.
4. Hobbies and leisure are an essential part of your lifestyle if you want to manage stress better.
5. Eating a healthy diet, with no long gaps between meals, and avoiding too much caffeine and refined sugar, will boost your chances of overcoming your stress.

5

Relax your body

In this chapter you will learn about physical relaxation and its importance in dealing with stress. You will be introduced to different relaxation exercises, varying in the time they take to complete.

What is relaxation?

Complete relaxation creates rest and calm, when your mind and body are entirely in balance, and totally at ease. As you relax, the muscles release tension, thinking becomes unhurried, and your body slows down. Autonomic arousal lowers to a low level to match the task of sitting or lying still, with no interaction with the outside world. You develop a feeling of warmth and a sense of wellbeing too.

When you relax, your body begins to move from a state of physiological arousal, geared up and ready for whatever action is required, to a state of physiological relaxation, where blood pressure, breathing and heart rate, and digestive functioning return to their relaxed state. Releasing muscle tension in itself can give relief from pain and discomfort. You could liken this to a row of soldiers, standing by and ready for action, being told 'At ease'.

So, when you relax:

▶ The body prepares for rest.

▶ Blood pressure decreases or stabilizes.

▶ Muscle tension decreases.

▶ Blood flow to muscles decreases.

▶ Blood flow to extremities increases.

▶ Pulse rate decreases.

▶ Brain relaxes.

▶ Breathing rate decreases.

▶ Breathing becomes less shallow.

▶ Anxiety levels decrease.

How do you feel?

Here are five key ideas from this chapter to think about now. They will be discussed later:

1 Are you ever aware that you are physically tense?

   a Occasionally

   b Sometimes

   c Often

   d Almost all the time

   e Never

   f Not sure

2 When you are tense, which parts of your body are mostly affected (note all that apply)?

   a Hands and arms

   b Shoulders

   c Face

   d Round the eyes

   e Scalp

   f Legs and feet

   g Back

   h Stomach

   i Other

3 Rest one hand flat on your tummy, just below your navel, and the other on your chest, just below the breastbone. Now just breathe away normally, but watch what happens to your hands. Does either move up and down as you breathe? Which moves the most?

4 Take a deep breath in, hold it for a second or two, then, as you slowly breathe out again, mentally scan your entire body and notice any areas which are tense. Make a note of these. Take another deep breath, hold it for a second or so, then slowly sigh it back out, this time allowing any tension you found to just release itself and drain away.

5 Which of these usually helps you to relax either at the time, or immediately afterwards (note all that apply)?

a Warm bath

b Running

c Cycling

d Walking

e Chatting to a friend

f Yoga

g Meditation

h Aerobics

i Watching TV

j Listening to music

k Partner giving you a neck rub or foot massage

l A nice meal

m Going out with friends

n Other

WHY YOU CAN'T JUST TELL YOURSELF TO RELAX

We've already explored how the part of our body that makes us relax, the autonomic nervous system or ANS, is the same part that makes us breathe and keeps our heart beating. It's sometimes likened to an 'automatic pilot'. Just as we can't tell our blood to circulate, or our stomach to digest our last meal, we can't tell our body or our mind to relax. The way to speak our body's language, and to communicate with both mind and body, is to use relaxation. This is something our body understands. And that's what this chapter will teach you.

DO YOU NEED SPECIAL RELAXATION TECHNIQUES?

For many people, simply going for a run, settling down to a good TV programme, polishing the car, or listening to your favourite music, is relaxing. This works for many people, depending on their personal interests and preferences, and having the time. Recent research has even discovered that stroking a friendly cat or dog, preferably of your own, has a noticeably calming effect.

But there are many situations when these everyday activities just don't work. If you are very stressed and anxious all the time, you can't always be going for a walk, or having a bath. What if you want to relax at the supermarket, or in a meeting at work? You have to get on with your life. Such activities are usually very time-consuming too. And if you're driving, or looking after children or an elderly person, what do you do then?

What is really needed is a way to relax within a minute or two, anywhere, anytime, without other people noticing. It is also good to be able to have a long, slow relaxation session, when time and space allow for this. Some of the 'Try it now' boxes in Chapters 1–4 have already introduced some of the quicker ways to relax. This chapter will provide more techniques for quick ways to relax, and also methods which you can enjoy for half an hour or more. We are all different, and there's no one size fits all about relaxation. So you can try out the various techniques and see what works best for you.

Relaxation is often referred to as 'exercise', making it sound like a very physical activity, needing energy and flexibility. Many think it's not for them. But this is not really the case. Rather than 'exercise', 'technique' or 'method' is much nearer to the reality of it. Most relaxation methods involve hardly any physical input, and none are at all strenuous. Many simply involve breathing or thinking.

So there should be something for everyone, and you don't have to be particularly fit for any of them. If you are at all concerned about any technique, just check with your doctor before you go ahead. Relaxation is not a difficult skill to learn – it's just about knowing how.

A FEW WORDS OF CAUTION WHEN USING RELAXATION TECHNIQUES

For the vast majority of people, relaxation should not present any problems for them, and provide nothing but benefits, with absolutely no side effects.

▶ Not strenuous

The most you are likely to be asked to do in any relaxation technique is tense a set of muscles – make a tight fist with your hand, for example. But if you are in any doubt at all about your fitness to use or try out a technique or method, then best not to go ahead with it. There will be lots of other alternatives offered, so you won't be missing out. Or you can adapt the activity to suit your particular needs. If it still works for you with your adaptation, then it is still going to be beneficial to you. It's as simple as that.

▶ High blood pressure

Care should be taken if you have raised blood pressure. In one or two of the techniques, there can be an initial increase in blood pressure brought about by tensing the muscles, so if this could be a problem for you, avoid methods which involve this.

▶ Tension up

A small minority of people may actually feel a bit more tense and anxious for the first few moments when trying out a technique involving relaxation or breathing exercises. This is caused by feeling anxious, unfamiliar or self-conscious about the techniques. Regular practice should sort out this difficulty fairly quickly, so don't be put off if it happens to you.

▶ Lowered awareness

As you would expect, the techniques given here may reduce your alertness and may even make you feel a little drowsy. Whilst trying out or using any of the relaxation techniques given in the book, and for around ten minutes afterwards, do not drive, operate machinery, stand up suddenly, or take part in any activity which requires full alertness.

Too much tension?

If stress means that for a lot of your day, your muscles are tenser than they really need to be, you'll probably have aches and pains, or tingling and numbness, especially in the neck, shoulders and back, usually in the evening when you relax, or next day. Unwanted muscle tension can even make some people feel off balance when standing or walking, as this can be caused by having more tension in one shoulder than in the other, or across your back, giving you an imbalance when you sit, stand or walk. This can feel very odd and unsettling.

THE BODY'S STRESS RESPONSE

The body is sophisticated and has been cleverly designed. In order to keep its systems all working as they should, and all pulling together, a series of chemical messengers have evolved over thousands of years. At any one time, countless chemical messengers are shuttling back and forth via the blood circulation all over the body, to reach a particular organ, and produce the necessary effects on it.

These chemical messengers are called hormones. You will probably be familiar with hormones such as oestrogen and testosterone, the sex hormones. But there are numerous other hormones, all with a specific job to do in the body. Adrenalin and cortisol are often called the 'stress hormones' and these are the messengers which create the changes in our bodies when we are stressed.

Everything begins in the brain, and though these parts of the brain have many other processes to look after, the main areas involved in the stress response are the hypothalamus and the pituitary gland. These are located deep inside the brain, but close to one another. The hypothalamus is roughly the shape and size of a pearl, and the pituitary gland, a pea-shaped structure, located just below it.

When we perceive what we feel to be a threat or danger, whether that be a golf ball heading for our head on the golf course, or an angry manager heading our way, the hypothalamus triggers the pituitary to secrete a specific hormone called adrenocorticotropic hormone, or ACTH, into the bloodstream. When this reaches the adrenal glands, small pyramid shaped organs located at the top of each kidney, this stimulates them to produce adrenalin and cortisol. It's all a kind of domino effect, with perceived stress acting as the starting pistol.

So during stress, the adrenal glands release adrenalin and cortisol into the blood stream, and as these chemical messengers travel around the body, they cause the heart to pump harder, open airways in the lungs, slow down the digestive process, increase blood flow to major muscle groups, and set in motion all the other functions needed for the body to fight or run to deal with the threat. As we saw earlier, this ancient mechanism evolved in prehistoric times, to deal with a physical threat, such as a sabre-tooth tiger, or a venomous snake, but can just as easily be triggered today by situations in which we feel threatened as a person. Some also argue that there is a third option in this process, 'fight, flight or freeze', because some people report that at times of fear or anxiety they experience a feeling of being 'frozen' or rooted to the spot, and completely unable to move. Many animals use this tactic to save their lives. The phrase 'stock still' describes the stillness of an animal which freezes as a safety mechanism, and blends into the background, to avert the stalker's gun.

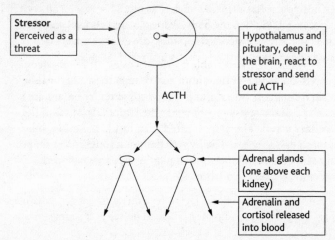

Brain waves

Another way of understanding relaxation is to use a completely different perspective from the chemistry of hormone messengers, which we've just been examining, and to investigate what is happening in terms of 'brain waves'.

In addition to the chemical processes working continually in the brain, you may be surprised to find that there is electrical activity going on in our brains all the time too. This is very low voltage activity, nothing like the strength of the domestic electrical supply we are familiar with. This electricity is described as a wave, because it isn't constant and even throughout the brain. It changes over our day from shallow and fast activity, like the ripples on the sea near the shore, to deeper and slower, like the sea waves far from the shore.

Wave name	Number every second (approx.)	Associated with
Delta	1–4	Deep sleep.
Theta	5–7	Just falling asleep.
Alpha	8–14	Relaxed but alert.Not working on any task in particular. Pleasant and relaxed feelings.
Beta	15–35	Very alert.Concentrating on a demanding task. Common during anxiety or panic attacks.
High Beta	27–35	Common during anxiety or panic attacks.

So as you see from the table above, if you want to relax you have to encourage the brain to move from producing mainly beta or high beta waves, to producing mainly alpha waves. You want to be relaxed, but still alert and awake. The experience of alpha waves is similar to meditation, and for most people, is more easily achieved with your eyes closed. If your eyes are open, you can still move into alpha by watching a scene such as waves lapping quietly on the seashore, or a beautiful and large scale landscape such as rolling hills, lakes or mountains. Exercise such as cycling, or running can also have this effect. Mindfulness techniques can also create these restful brain wave patterns (more on this in Chapter 9). You can also use a specialist DVD, or computer program to simulate these for you. There is a wide range of merchandise currently available to help with this (see Chapter 13).

Similarly, when you want to get to sleep, you should start off by using relaxation to help you to achieve alpha waves. This allows you to wind down slowly from the beta and high beta waves which are keeping you awake, slowly into alpha, and then if you continue relaxing ever more deeply, into theta, and then into the welcome delta waves of deep and refreshing sleep. Trying to move straight from beta to delta is too much to ask of your brain, as many parents of young children will agree.

Learning to relax – making a start

The most fundamental and effective of all the stress management techniques, is relaxation. It has two very powerful effects:

1 Relaxing your body is one of the best ways to reduce the arousal that stress can cause.

2 Relaxing often also has the added benefit of 'damping down' your body's reaction to stress in the first place, and improving your resilience.

So there are two top-notch reasons for learning this important skill. Just like learning any new skill, you have to practise a bit to become good at it. Imagine trying to ride a bike, play the piano or drive a car without having practised first – but once you've learned it, you never forget it. It doesn't take long to learn how to relax. Usually a few repeats will get you there.

 Mythbuster

If you've tried relaxation like this before and it didn't work, don't be put off – if it didn't work, you were doing it wrong, so give it another chance! We'll show you the right way to do it here.

▶ Ten Steps Relaxation (about 15 minutes)

1. Find a quiet spot where you won't be disturbed.

↓

2. You can either lie down or sit comfortably with your head supported for this.

↓

3. Make sure you are warm and comfortable. You might find a warm blanket useful as you can feel a little cold when you relax.

↓

4. If you think you might fall asleep when you relax, make your session earlier in the day.

↓

5. What you will be doing here is not at all strenuous, but does involve tensing your muscles. Read it through first, and as soon as you are familiar with the technique, close your eyes whilst practising, as this is usually much more effective.

↓

6. Lie or sit comfortably, head supported if possible.

↓

7. Deliberately make a fist and tense up both hands really hard for five or six seconds...hold it...now let the tension go.

↓

8. Slowly repeat this for each of the following parts of your body in turn:

▶ arms

▶ shoulders

▶ neck and head

▶ face

▶ back and chest

- tummy and bottom
- legs, feet and toes.

9. Relax for a few moments/minutes – more if you have time.

10. Rouse yourself gradually.

 ## Remember this

International Stress Management Association (ISMA) UK says that 'a good relaxation technique is a weapon that you always carry with you, to help you deal with any situation as it arises. Make relaxation a regular part of your daily routine. There are so many relaxation techniques, from deep-breathing and visualization to meditation and self-hypnosis. Find one that works for you.'

RAPID RELAXATION*

If you feel that you're relaxing well with 'Ten Steps Relaxation' and perhaps becoming a little impatient or bored following the instructions, then you're ready to move on to use faster methods. You'll find one of these below. You should move on to using it now. This is called Rapid Relaxation (there are two others in Optional extras).

Try as many of these as you want, and choose one which you prefer or that works best for you, to use regularly. Or you might like to vary which one you use from day to day. You can still use Ten Steps Relaxation whenever you want if you enjoy the longer session. As soon as you master any of these methods, you can use them whenever and wherever you feel stressed.

- ### Rapid Relaxation Technique 1
1 Lie or sit comfortably, eyes closed, and allow your breathing to become slow and even.

2 Now concentrate on your hands and arms – *don't tense them* – and concentrate on letting all the tension drain away from them.

↓

3 Continue concentrating like this on each part of your body in turn, (same order as for Ten Steps Relaxation – hands and arms, shoulders, neck and head, face, back and stomach, legs and feet), letting all the tension drain away, *without tensing them first.*

Enjoy the feeling of relaxation you have produced for a few moments or minutes.

↓

4 When you feel ready, finish your session gradually. In your own time, with no rush, allow yourself to become more alert… Have a yawn and a stretch if you feel like it…When you feel alert, return quietly to what you were doing.

PARTIAL RELAXATION

So far you've learned how to relax the whole body, all at once. But what if you are using all or part of your body to do something, like walking, driving, shopping, talking on the phone, or using a computer or a till? You couldn't do any of these if your entire body was relaxed. How do you keep the rest of your body relaxed whilst you are using part of it?

People often find that they are very tense when carrying out everyday tasks, and can find themselves using far more tension than needed in everyday tasks. Many people grip the phone or their coffee cup far too tightly, hold facial muscles taught when talking to people, arch their back when driving, or experiencing neck or back pain from tension when using a computer or supermarket check-out till.

The answer to this is to learn 'Partial Relaxation'. But first, check where you are with the other methods:

If you are still finding you need to use Ten Steps Relaxation to relax fully, then continue with this every day, but now try 'Partial Relaxation' to see how you get on. Move onto Rapid Relaxation now too, and give it a try.

If you have moved on to practising with Rapid Relaxation, continue to use this every day, but also now try out 'Partial Relaxation' to see how you get on.

Whatever stage you're at, try practising with Partial Relaxation every other day.

Here's what to do for 'Partial Relaxation':

Use any method you like to become very relaxed.

Lying or sitting, eyes closed, begin by moving your hands in the air as if say, typing, writing or whatever. Try to *keep the rest of your body completely relaxed* as you do this. Continue doing this for a few moments.

Now open your eyes slowly, and look around keeping your head still. Move your eyes only, and again, try to keep the *rest of your body relaxed* and at ease.

↓

Next, look around further by moving your head a little, again, keeping the rest of your body relaxed. Now, keep your head and eyes still, and try saying a few words, again keeping your body relaxed. Now relax completely again for a few moments.

↓

Now try sitting up, eyes open, totally relaxed for a few moments. Now stand up *slowly*, and see if you can stand in a totally relaxed way. After standing still for a few moments, walk around a little, pick something up and carry it, then replace it – all the time keeping relaxed any part of your body not in use, with the minimum of tension required for those in use.

Now lie or sit back down again, and relax your whole body completely for some moments/minutes. Finish the session as you would for Rapid or Total Relaxation.

BREATHE TO RELAX

We've already seen how your breathing can be affected by stress. Breathing takes in the body's fuel, and disposes of some of its waste products. So if we upset its rhythm, it's easy to see how the body's delicate balance can be disturbed, and we experience this as unexpected physical and mental symptoms. Anxiety about these feelings just makes you more stressed. This increased breathing rate, brought about by stress, is best relieved by breathing exercises which can re-establish normal breathing rhythms. There are many approaches to this. Here are just two of them to start you off – Sleep-style Breathing, which has a very relaxing effect, and Alert-style Breathing which returns breathing to normal, but maintains alertness. It's better to begin by learning Sleep-style Breathing.

SLEEP-STYLE BREATHING (TAKES ABOUT 5 MINUTES)

Stress makes us breathe faster, and mainly with the upper chest, which you can see moving. This is less efficient, causing hyperventilation, and can also fill up the lungs, making you feel as if you can't take a breath. When we're asleep, we use all of our lungs, and use the muscles in the tummy or abdomen to breathe, and you can see these muscles moving if you look at someone who is asleep, or a sleeping animal. If you can breathe the way you do when you're asleep, this can have a very calming, relaxing and yet energizing effect.

▶ Lie or sit in a comfortable well supported chair.

▶ Rest one flat hand gently just below your navel, the other on your upper chest, about level with your underarms.

▶ Let your breath go, then breathe in slowly and very gently – allowing your tummy to swell up like a swelling balloon, lifting your hand.

▶ In your own time, breathe out again gently, and notice your tummy fall again.

▶ Continue this gentle breathing, trying to have as little movement of your upper chest as you can.

With practice you will manage to breathe in this way without using your hands, and you can use it to help you get off to sleep.

ALERT-STYLE BREATHING (TAKES A MINUTE OR TWO, FOUR OR FIVE TIMES A DAY)

If you want to introduce normal breathing patterns with a less calming effect, there are many techniques which can be used when you want to be relaxed, but alert too. Here are some simple breathing techniques which you can use anytime. Thousands of people have found techniques like this can be a life-line, as they are so quick and easy to do when needed during a stressful day. You'll also find more of these throughout the book in some of the 'Try it now' boxes.

There are always spare minutes in the day which we can use for this – waiting for a bus or a taxi, on the bus or train, queuing at the shops for your lunchtime sandwich, or to pay your petrol, whatever. Even the busiest of people have these spare moments – they can sometimes be the moments which make us most stressed as we are in a hurry and have been made to wait, so what better use to put them to, when there's nothing we can do about the delay?

See which of these or the others in the book work best for you. Then practise your favourites for a minute or two each day until you can use them whenever you need them to help you to relax and cope better. All of the techniques can be done unseen whenever you need to relax. Spending a minute or two relaxing like this, four or five times a day, has the added bonus of keeping your stress level down throughout the day.

1 Full body scan:

   a Take a gentle breath in, and as you're doing this silently scan your whole body for any tense areas, starting from your toes, and working upwards.

   b As you breathe out, relax any tension you found.

   Repeat a and b

2 Reverse count:

   a Focus on your breathing for a few moments.

   b Begin counting down silently from 10 to 0, saying the next number silently each time you breathe out.

3 Cutting your tension strings:

Let your breath go, then slowly take in a deep breath, filling your entire chest, so that your shoulders are lifted, and your head is erect...hold it for around five seconds...then let your breath go with a big sigh of relief, dropping your shoulders and slumping your whole body like a puppet whose strings have just been cut.

Repeat (once only).

4 Easy as 1-2-3:

▶ Lie or sit comfortably, with good support.

▶ Let your breath go, then take a gentle breath in to your own slow silent count of 1...2...3... then breathe out again in your own time to your own slow and silent count of 1...2...3....

▶ Continue gently breathing to this rhythm for a minute or so.

Aids to relaxation

Many people have tried out a stress dot or a stress card, temperature strip, or similar relaxation aid. These work through contact with the skin, and are based on measuring skin temperature which tends to be lower when stressed or tense, because the stress response reduces blood flow to the peripheries such as feet and hands. Also, when you are stressed there is an increase in muscle tension, the blood vessels near the skin's surface constrict and the temperature of your hands and feet decreases. So when you relax, your hands and feet become warmer as blood flow returns. The colour change of the stress dot or stress card, simply but visually demonstrates the changes in the body's stress levels. You place the dot on the fleshy part of the joint between the first finger and thumb on the back of the hand. The inside of the wrist or the forehead can also provide an effective reading. So if a group of people all have stress dots on their foreheads during a meeting, they can all see what's happening to each other's stress levels, but not their own. But you can use this kind of 'bio-feedback' for yourself, to become aware of when you are becoming stressed, and this usually acts as a trigger to let go of tension and relax. You can quickly become quite skilful at doing this.

There are also 'tactile' stress or desk toys which give the hands something to do, for example squeezing, stretching or 'squidging', and this can have a relaxing effect for many people. The rhythmic and repetitive movement of some 'executive toys' has a similar relaxing effect. A nodding bird descending slowly down a branch or Newton's cradle (six metal balls swinging in a rhythmic pattern), are typical examples. All of these effects can now be reproduced on a computer, and there are numerous software packages available. This will be explored further in Chapter 13.

Music and other sounds can work well for some people, and research bears this out. The choice is a very personal thing, with style and type of music or whether whale sound or a gurgling brook, being very much down to personal taste, and simply what works for you.

The main drawback of 'stress aids' is that most of them can't be used while you're actually working, or if you're on the go – imagine juggling during a business meeting, or at an interview! However, they are fun and something a little different. Every way of relaxing has its time and place.

Focus points

1. The brain sends two chemical messengers through the body in the blood to prepare you to deal with a stressor. These are called adrenalin and cortisol.
2. There are numerous relaxation techniques to try out, and choose from. Some are long and slow, some can be done quickly, in a few seconds.
3. When you relax your whole body deeply, you'll have minimal muscle tension, your heart and breathing rates will decrease, and you'll feel good.
4. A muscle will relax if you first deliberately place it under tension, and then release that tension.
5. The brain has waves of electrical activity which change in response to relaxation. Waves known as alpha waves are experienced when we are relaxed but alert.

6

Relax your mind

So far we've been focussing almost exclusively on relaxing the body. We've already met some relaxation and breathing techniques in Chapter 5. But sometimes it's relaxing the mind which is the stumbling block. Even if you've succeeded in unwinding all your muscles, thoughts can still be falling over one another inside your head, from the mundane to the nerve-racking. In this chapter you'll learn how to relax your mind.

Relax your mind as well as your body

Being able to relax physically is an important first step, and will go a long way to helping your mind to relax, but sometimes a bit more help is needed. The vital point about relaxing the mind is to be aware that just telling yourself not to think about something, or trying to take your mind off your worries won't achieve a thing. The more you try to do this, sometimes the worse it becomes. Why? Because the more you do this the more you are actually paying attention to, and concentrating on, your worries. Sometimes they can even assume even greater proportion and seem much larger than they really are, simply because you keep concentrating on them so much.

How do you feel?

Here are five key ideas from this chapter to think about now. They will be discussed later:

1 How much of the time is your mind relaxed (select all that apply)?

   a Most of the time

   b Hardly ever

   c Some of the time

   d When I'm asleep

   e Not even when I'm asleep, as I have frightening dreams

   f Never

2 If your mind isn't relaxed, what is it doing? (Choose all that apply.)

   a Going over and over things

   b Being negative

   c Feeling guilty

   d Self-blaming

e Blaming other people

   f Won't focus on what I want it to

   g Worrying

   h Just won't stop

   i Racing

   j Exaggerating

   k Don't know

3 How good at calming and relaxing your mind would you say you were most days?

   a Can't do it at all

   b Not good

   c Quite good

   d Very good

   e Find it easy

   f Other

4 When trying to calm your mind, which of these have you tried to do (choose all that apply)?

   a Empty your mind

   b Think of nothing

   c Meditation

   d Keep busy with other things

   e Focus on a relaxing word or image

   f None of these

   g Other

5 How well do you sleep? (Choose all that apply.)

   a Don't know

   b Very well most nights

   c Fairly well most nights

   d Varies from night to night

   e Poorly most nights

   f Very poorly most nights

   g Hardly get any sleep most nights

   h Difficult getting to sleep

   i Wake up early and can't get back to sleep

   j Other

Lifestyle and the mind

When it comes to having a calm and relaxed mind, free from unnecessary worries and concerns, the first place to start is with your lifestyle. Chapter 4 showed how lifestyle holds the key to much of today's stress, and covered many ways of improving things through fairly straightforward changes. Stress is like that. Fairly simple changes can have big rewards.

So taking breaks, and making sure you have meaningful and enjoyable time for yourself, will go a long way to allowing a busy, tired mind to slow down. Being sure of your priorities, and managing time effectively are also going to make a difference, as will getting enough sleep, exercise and healthy food inside you.

With all of that in place, part of the job will be done. All of your tactics work together to produce a good end result. The other part is to learn to use simple techniques to relax your mind, and you can start doing this now.

HOW TO TALK TO YOUR MIND

For many people, it's easier to relax their body than their mind. Physical relaxation will calm the mind to a varying extent, but often the worries, concerns and what-ifs are still nagging away, sometimes quietly, and sometimes loudly. So some special techniques for relieving these kinds of problems can be particularly helpful.

Just for a moment, try this:

Imagine in your mind's eye, as clearly as you can, an elephant. See its shape, its skin, huge feet, flapping ears and trunk. Do you have that image? Focus on it with your whole mind for about 20 seconds.

Now, stop thinking about the elephant. Dismiss it from your mind completely. Don't think about the elephant any more. Don't see the elephant's huge feet, or trunk, or the elephant's small eyes. Stop thinking about the elephant...What are you seeing now? For most people, they'll still be seeing the elephant, probably more clearly and bigger than before. And it's like that with your worries too. The more you tell yourself to stop thinking about them, the more that reminds you to continue to think about them, and the bigger and more detailed they become in your mind. So what to do?

What to do is to focus your mind on something else. It's almost impossible for your mind to think of nothing, so you have to give it what it needs – something else to think about. And if that something else is pleasant and relaxing, so much the better.

So now, imagine in your mind's eye, a bowl full of your favourite fruits. See the bowl clearly, and fill it with the fruits you enjoy the most. Fill it all with the same fruit, or as many fruits as you like, all juicy and ready to eat, just the way you like them. See the colours, the textures. Smell the ripeness. Imagine the juiciness. Have you got an image? Is it fruit or is it an elephant? Is your mouth watering?

Even if you're not the best at creating images in your mind's eye, and you didn't have clear pictures there, you should have experienced enough to form an idea of how this was working, and what a good way to relax the mind this can be.

Remember this

There are two key tips here:

1 The best way to take your mind off your worries is to give it something else to think about.

2 And the way to make it relax is to give it something relaxing to think about.

Lots of suggestions on exactly how to go about this are given throughout this chapter and elsewhere in the book. Try them out and see what works best for you. Everyone is different and will find some work better than others. This is probably truer of relaxing the mind than relaxing the body. People find they have particular preferences, which is wholly understandable. It's a bit like choosing a comfortable easy chair. Also, it's a new skill, and needs a bit of practice. So, give it time, and practise a bit. The rewards are well worth it! Here are some to get you started.

WAYS TO RELAX YOUR MIND

Before trying to relax your mind, first use whatever method you have found so far is working best for you to relax your body, preferably one of the shorter ones. Use a long slow method if you want to, as it's important that your body is relaxed. As you get more skilled, you'll be able to relax your body in a few minutes, or less, and then move onto your mind.

Now try out these methods to see what works best for you. When you've done this, you can use that method, straightaway after the type of physical relaxation technique you're practising every day, to give a way of relaxing both mind and body together. You can also use these techniques on their own anytime at all.

▶ *Imagine 1*

First, take time to relax your body. Then, close your eyes and for about a minute, picture in your mind as clearly and in as much detail as you can ONE of these calming scenes:

▷ tall yellow corn swaying in the summer breeze

▷ water trickling over the pebbles in a stream

▷ branches blowing in the breeze

▷ boats bobbing in the harbour

▷ waves lapping onto the sea shore

▷ a circle of dark deep green velvet.

▶ *Imagine 2*

First, take time to relax your body. Now, in your mind's eye, for about a minute focus absolutely on ONE of these:

▷ a well-loved face

▷ a calming poem

▷ a relaxing prayer

▷ well-loved picture.

▶ *Imagine 3*

First, take time to relax your body. Then, *for about a minute* repeat silently (or softly out loud) and very slowly a word, sound, or phrase such as:

▷ r...e...l...a...x...

▷ all...is...well....

▷ let...tranquillity...ease...my...mind...

▷ peaceful...and...calm....

▷ I...feel...calmness...within...

▷ completely safe...completely calm...

▷ so...hum...

▷ other words which you find calming...

HOW DID YOU GET ON?

What's important in stress management is to try different methods to come up with something which suits, and then practise the skill often to make improvements just like learning to drive, or use a new mobile phone. Perseverance pays off.

You will need a bit of time to try out the various options. Creative people often find it much easier to imagine scenes or pictures. Words and phrases can be easier for most people. Was this true for you? This is a very new skill, and it may seem a bit unusual. But it is definitely the way to calm a busy, tired mind that just won't stop going over and over the same ground, until you're exhausted. You'll definitely find it gets better and better the more often you try it, and you'll gain more and more benefit too. People around you will notice the difference.

Thinking yourself stressed

This is the old idea of whether we see the glass as half-full or half-empty. The belief that the way we think can make all the difference to how we feel. This topic was flagged up earlier in the book, but there is so much more to learn. We all know someone who sees the positive and won't give up no matter what, and others who go to pieces and give up hope at the first hurdle. Then there are people who remain cheerful and determined no matter what life throws at them – and others who can always find something to grumble about. What makes them different is how they think about what happens to them. The difference is in their attitude to life – their general disposition, their outlook and their expectations. Albert Schweitzer, a 20th-century European philosopher, put it well when he said that we can change our lives, simply by changing our attitudes.

So it's all about attitude, and how we habitually think about our world. Most people probably fit somewhere in between the two extremes already mentioned. We pick up our thinking style and attitudes mainly during our upbringing and other experiences in life. Watch a toddler when something unusual or different happens – an unexpected visitor, sudden noise, or if they spill their drink. They immediately look at their carer to see how to react. Is this a happy, welcome event, an annoying or frightening occurrence, or something to just ignore as if it doesn't matter? They learn this from their carers just as they learn how to dress themselves or use a spoon. How our thinking processes operate is also thought to be at least partly inherited.

So to beat stress, thinking and attitudes are a part of the picture that cannot be ignored. It pays to consider how you think, and the kind of conversations or 'inner dialogue' you're having in your head every day. We all have a kind of 'running commentary' going on in our heads, and this can often be negative and discouraging. If a person's inner dialogue contains frequent phrases such as some of the following, they may be creating problems and stress for themselves:

▶ I ought to get this done.

▶ This is all too much for me.

▶ It's not fair.

▶ I must not make a mistake.

▶ She's useless.

▶ It won't work.

▶ This is awful.

▶ I know I can't cope with this.

▶ What will people think?

Thinking like this isn't an illness, it's just a habit. It's easy to pick up this negative style of thinking, especially if we hear a lot of it around us. But it does increase our chance of feeling stressed. The good news is that how we think is not fixed for life. It can be changed. Chapter 7 will explain much more about this, and how you can make the changes needed to beat stress.

RELAXING YOUR MOUTH AND EYES CAN WORK WONDERS
Whenever we are thinking or imagining, you probably haven't noticed, but our eyes, mouth and tongue make very tiny

movements. They may be tiny, but they are there. As we think, we use words, so the muscles of speech make tiny movements. If we imagine we are doing something involving looking around, the muscles of sight will also make tiny movements.

Your eye movements can be more noticeable than those of your mouth and tongue, which tend to be tinier, but both come into action whenever you are thinking or imagining. And if you have a busy, hurried and pressurized mind, your eyes, mouth and tongue will also be involved in a small way.

So maybe, if you try not to make these movements, you can reduce the amount of activity in your brain, and relax your mind. Test this out for yourself now. Read what to do first, then try it with eyes closed.

While you are following these instructions, pay close attention to your eyes, mouth, lips and tongue:

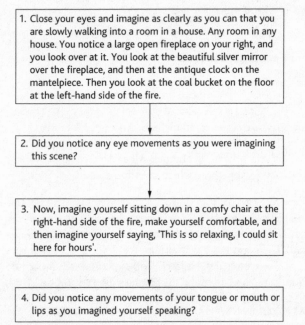

1. Close your eyes and imagine as clearly as you can that you are slowly walking into a room in a house. Any room in any house. You notice a large open fireplace on your right, and you look over at it. You look at the beautiful silver mirror over the fireplace, and then at the antique clock on the mantelpiece. Then you look at the coal bucket on the floor at the left-hand side of the fire.

2. Did you notice any eye movements as you were imagining this scene?

3. Now, imagine yourself sitting down in a comfy chair at the right-hand side of the fire, make yourself comfortable, and then imagine yourself saying, 'This is so relaxing, I could sit here for hours'.

4. Did you notice any movements of your tongue or mouth or lips as you imagined yourself speaking?

Try it now

When you want to relax your mind, pay particular attention to relaxing the muscles of speech and sight. This can be surprisingly effective.

Sounds can be relaxing too*

We've all heard the term 'easy listening', and there are radio stations such as 'Smooth Radio' or 'Magic' which only play music which most people would find easy on the ear, and quite relaxing, in a general sense. According to psychologist Dr David Lewis, the composers of Baroque music have created music which generates the brain wave mixture we experience in 'relaxed awareness'. Our choice of music for unwinding and relaxing is a very personal matter, and has much to do with associations built up over a lifetime. The Four Tops singing 'I'll be There', takes me right back to happy summer days in school, every time I hear it. Marie Osmond singing 'Paper Roses' immediately evokes my local football team winning the Scottish Knock-Out Cup on a sunny May day at Glasgow's Hampden Park. Popular (pop) music has been said to form the soundtrack to your life.

The right choice of music can do everything from slowing heart rate to producing endorphins. Well-known examples of music which encourages relaxation include 'Air on the G String' by Bach, 'Pastoral' by Beethoven, 'Nocturne in G Minor' by Chopin, 'Water Music' by Handel. All easily available, here are some other types of music which are thought to be relaxing for most people:

▶ Gregorian chants

▶ pan pipes

▶ Baroque music (e.g. Handel, Bach, Vivaldi)

▶ any music whose tempo coincides with average resting heart rate of 60 beats per minute.

Certain types of music can comfort a crying baby. Lullabies have worked on this exact principle for thousands of years. Many young babies are soothed by the sound of vacuuming or a hairdryer, or their mother's favourite music, possibly because they associate these with the calmness and security of the womb, where they would regularly hear these sounds. Many expectant parents now deliberately play certain tracks or styles of music frequently, so that this music is likely to soothe the baby after it is born. The sounds imagined to be heard by the baby in the womb, such as a human heartbeat and circulating blood, are available on CD or for download, to help the new baby sleep.

Sounds other than music can also exert a calming influence. Birdsong, a babbling brook, or the slow click of a metronome are typical examples. Some sounds can be more relaxing than others, though this is again open to personal preference. For some people, the sound of silence is particularly peaceful. For myself, I grew up in a busy household, and find silence strangely uninviting, but can relax easily with a buzz of background noise going on. I find writing in silence almost impossible, and always have some music in the background. As a student, I had the same experience, and could only study with Radio One playing. I find whale sounds mildly irritating, and not at all relaxing, but for others it's breathtakingly peaceful and evocative. So music and sound is very individual and personal, but what we hear has a profound effect on our mood and ability to relax. Shops know the kind of music to play to us to encourage us to linger longer in their aisles, and to encourage us to make a purchase.

CDs and downloads to use as a relaxation aid are now available with every sound you can imagine. Sometimes the sounds and the music we find most relaxing are those we associate with happy or relaxing experiences. This is also true of fragrances or smells. Most people find the smell of baking bread, bacon sizzling on the hob, salty sea air, or freshly mown grass can transport them to happy times. Aromatherapy builds on this idea, and will be discussed later in Chapter 11. Many of the techniques for relaxing the mind given earlier in this chapter also use this principle.

SOUND AND IMAGERY TOGETHER

Combining sound and imagery can be a powerful combination for most people. The brain is almost fooled into believing you are really experiencing what you're seeing and hearing. After all, our body and mind are from the Stone Age, when audio and video recording just didn't exist. Your personal choice of relaxing sounds combined with relaxing imagery can be extremely effective. There will be more on this in Chapter 13, which looks at how the internet and modern technology can be used to provide this kind of relaxation experience.

TRY IT FOR YOURSELF

Here are just some of the sounds or imagery, or both, available on CD, or as DVDs, from specialist suppliers, gift shops, garden centres, or for download on-line. Most give you the opportunity to test them out first, to be sure they are going to work for you.

- summer sounds – birds twittering, light breeze, branches swaying

- waves crashing on the seashore

- leaves blowing gently in the breeze

- gurgling river

- cat purring

- birdsong, dolphin song, whalesong

- a babbling brook

- waterfall flowing over rocks

- sounds of spring – lambs bleating, spring birdsong.

GUIDED IMAGERY*

It is also possible and surprisingly easy to produce imagery and sound completely from the imagination. This is called guided imagery, and can be done entirely using your own imagination to bring to mind calming images and sounds. As with CDs and DVDs of sounds and imagery, the brain can hardly tell the difference, so this can give a tremendously relaxing break from your stressful day, and can be achieved anywhere, anytime, and with no special equipment.

Remember this

In guided imagery, build in lots of detail, and experience your surroundings as vividly as you can. Make what's in your imagination suit you. Make it yours. Hear the sounds, see the images, feel the sensations, smell the air around you, feel the sun on your skin. Most people need a little practice to get the full effect. Start by spending just a minute or two in your imagined place, then build this up gradually to a session length which suits you.

Here's what to do.

Read over the scenario described below. You can make a recording of the description if that is easier. There are others in 'Optional extras' to try if you prefer, or for another time.

When you're happy you know what to do, settle back somewhere comfortable and relax your body as much as possible, using any technique which works for you.

Then gently close your eyes, and begin to gradually develop a picture of yourself in your mind's eye, in ONE of the following settings, in as much detail and as vividly as you can. Use all your senses to feel, hear, smell and touch.

Summer stream:

Sitting or lying, warm and comfortable by a gurgling stream on a warm summer's afternoon in the country… hear the birds singing in the trees…the leaves fluttering in the gentle breeze which flows softly over you…and feel the warm sun on your skin…or the water on your toes as you dip them in the clear, warm water….

Silver light:

Standing, lying, or sitting…comfortable, safe and warm… from high above you, a shower of soft sparkling silver light begins to fall unhurriedly in a never-ending stream…soothing… warm…and so refreshing…cleansing every part of your mind and soul…the shower is washing away all of your tension…all stress…freeing you from all cares and concerns…softly washing all of these away from your body…and then vanishing down into the ground beneath you…

Your favourite place:

In your own special safe place...you choose...anywhere you feel safe and calm...where are you?...what do you hear?...what are you doing?...sensations?...

Take as long as you like to visualize, then when you feel ready, slowly let the image go, and gradually begin to pay attention to your breathing again, and your surroundings. Allow yourself to become more and more aware, until you are fully aware and alert again.

Meditation*

Meditation is actually a simple process, and doesn't need to be associated with a religion or spiritual belief system. Various forms of meditation have been practised in many parts of the world for thousands of years. In the 21st century industrialized world, we often have spiritual or religious associations with meditation, and imagine religious people sitting in awkward or uncomfortable positions for long periods.

But meditative techniques don't need to have these associations. They are simple and straightforward procedures, which can produce deep relaxation, alpha brain waves, and a very restful state of mind. According to Professor Patricia Carrington, from New Jersey, meditation produces a deep physiological relaxation, similar to deep sleep, but we remain awake.

Mythbuster

You don't have to wear anything special, be a member of a special religious group, or sit with legs crossed to meditate. It's a basic human skill anyone can learn.

The techniques here draw on the basics of meditation, with any associations with religions or philosophies stripped away, leaving it in its purest form. So they should be suitable for all readers. However, if you want to follow this up and explore the broader subject of meditation, and its links, you'll find some jumping-off points and other reference materials in Optional extras in Appendices 1 and 2, at the end of the book.

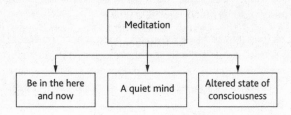

When people meditate, they are aiming to achieve three things: a quiet mind, being in the here and now, and an 'altered state of consciousness'. This 'altered state of consciousness' isn't as 'out there' as it sounds. This just means we feel different from the way we feel when we are going about our everyday business. It's a quieter, more centred, peaceful and grounded level, the sort of way you might feel out in the countryside on a sunny day, or out in the hills, or sitting on a quiet beach watching the waves lapping in and out. So, though it is an 'altered' state, it is still a 'normal' state. It is a state we are all capable of achieving. It's similar to the deep relaxation, and alpha brain waves we've already described.

HOW OFTEN SHOULD YOU MEDITATE?

Every day, for 15–20 minutes is a good baseline to work from. Don't overdo it, as more than this can begin to reverse its beneficial effects, or produce unwanted emotional experiences. It is best to stick to one, or at most two 15–20 minutes sessions of meditation a day.

HOW TO MEDITATE

The aim is to meditate for 15–20 minutes every day, sitting comfortably, somewhere quiet and peaceful if you can. Before making a start, relaxing music or sounds to suit your taste can be used to set a thoughtful and tranquil mood. Again, it's a matter of taste, but you can continue with your preferred sound during meditation to enhance the experience.

In order to meditate successfully, all you need to do is sit quietly, and concentrate entirely on a word, a sound, a picture or image, or other point of focus. This ties in with an earlier point about calming a busy mind being most easily achieved by thinking about something else, something which is calming and relaxing. Some meditations suggest laying your point of focus onto your breathing rhythm; for example, placing 'so' on the inward breath and 'hum' on the outward.

If you want to meditate by focussing on a word, phrase, short poem or sound, this is known as a *mantra*. A picture or image is known as a *mandala*, and is often circular, or has circles within it, as mandala means circle in the ancient language, Sanskrit. If you have a faith or belief system which involves praying, you can pray whilst meditating, as an alternative to using a mantra, or mandala. The first important step before starting to learn to meditate is to decide whether to begin with a mantra or mandala.

Remember this

If your attention wanders when meditating, as it certainly will at first, don't give up. What to do is just notice quietly what has happened, and then simply and gently return your thoughts to your point of focus. Like most relaxation techniques, some practice is likely to be needed, and you'll gradually be able to meditate for longer without being distracted. Have patience and give it time. It is well worth it.

▶ Choosing a mantra*

Any word or phrase, in any language can be used as a mantra. If you go to a meditation class, a list of these will be provided by the teacher for you to choose from. A mantra should sound resonant and soothing. Phrases in English, such as 'Slow down' or 'Let go' can be used, and are sometimes called 'affirmations'. Here are some short mantras and affirmations:

▶ calm

▶ Shi-rim

▶ one

▶ peaceful and quiet

▶ Om

▶ Om...namah...shivaya...(sounded 'om numaa shivaa-yuh' and means 'I honour my own inner state' in Sanskrit).

▶ Choosing a mandala*

The picture or image you choose for your mandala should be calming and pleasing to the eye. Try out any of these you feel works for you:

- ▶ a picture or tapestry of a highly patterned and vibrantly coloured circle is a common mandala

- ▶ a flickering candle

- ▶ a loved one's face

- ▶ an open water lily on a pond.

▶ How to meditate using a mantra

Choose one of the mantras or affirmations (or one from 'Optional extras', or one of your own).

Make yourself comfortable, in a sitting position. You're aiming to relax deeply, without falling asleep.

Play some relaxing music or sounds if you find this helpful, and give yourself time to begin to unwind slowly. Allow your mind, breathing and thinking to begin to slow down too. No pressure. Just let it happen in its own time.

Read the remaining instructions (below), and when you're ready, try it.

Begin by saying your mantra quietly, but with no effort, stretching its sound slowly and rhythmically, for several repeats. Then when you feel ready, whisper it – and then when it feels right, think it silently to yourself. Finally, think it silently with your eyes closed. You can continue to repeat the mantra out loud (chant) if you prefer.

If your attention wanders, don't be concerned about this – simply and gently return your thoughts to the mantra.

Slowly build up from meditating in this way for a few seconds at a session, to at most 15–20 minutes once or twice a day.

▶ How to meditate using a mandala

Choose one of the above mandalas, or an image of your own (or one from 'Optional extras'). You can meditate by focussing on the actual object, or a picture of the object, or by imagining the mandala in your mind's eye.

Make yourself comfortable, in a sitting position. You're aiming to relax deeply, without falling asleep.

Play some relaxing music or sounds if you find this helpful, and give yourself time to begin to unwind slowly. Allow your mind, breathing and thinking to begin to slow down too. No pressure. Just let it happen in its own time.

Read the remaining instructions (below), and when you're ready, try it.

Begin by bringing your attention to your mandala. Close your eyes when you feel ready if your mandala is imagined. With no rush, and without forcing it, just allow your attention to slowly leave everything else behind, as you focus completely on the mandala's every detail – textures, shape, colour, light, shade and movement.

If your attention wanders, don't be concerned – simply and gently return your thoughts to the mandala.

Slowly build up from meditating in this way for a few seconds at a session, to at most 15–20 minutes once or twice a day.

MINI-MEDITATIONS WORK TOO

If you don't have much time, you can still make meditation work for you. According to Professor Carrington, what she calls 'mini-meditations' can be very effective. So if you can fit several shorter sessions into your day, each lasting two to three minutes, this will bring great benefits. For active, busy people, this can be especially worthwhile, and can be particularly good at keeping tension levels under control over your day. There are many 'windows' of two or three minutes in most people's days, into which quick relaxation techniques like this fit very neatly – break times at work, waiting for a taxi, or a bus or train, before the others arrive for a meeting or phone or video conference, standing at the photocopier, waiting to see the dentist, and so on.

GETTING A GOOD NIGHT'S SLEEP

It is often said that we can cope with anything during the day, if we can just get a good night's sleep. I think I would agree with that. And sometimes it's an impossible dream, if you have small children, or care for someone who is elderly or disabled. But if stress is keeping you from a restful sleep, or a poor sleep pattern is making the day stressful, here are some ideas for making sure you get your sleep:

▶ Noise

Quiet is essential for most people, though you can become used to almost anything. You can use earplugs if there is a lot of noise from the street or from neighbours, or if you have to sleep during the day.

▶ Showers

Keep your shower till the morning. A shower just before you turn in will revive you too much.

▶ Dinner

A big meal in the evening will discourage sleep at bedtime. Try a light dinner no later than 6:30 p.m. But no need to go to bed hungry. If you are hungry before bed, have an oaty cereal or cereal bar, a milky drink, or some honey; this should improve your night's sleep, as these foods are all known to increase levels of the brain chemical tryptophan, which is thought to produce deeper sleep.

▶ Draw the curtains or blinds

Darkness encourages sleep, and the release of melatonin, a hormone produced when we sleep. Black-out blinds or curtains can work wonders, especially for summer early morning sunrises.

▶ Sleeping conditions

Rather like Goldilocks' porridge, your bedroom needs to be not too hot, and not too cool. Your mattress should be not too soft, not too hard. It shouldn't be too old either. The bed should offer comfortable support, and enough room, especially if you're a couple. Use breathable fabrics for your bedclothes, and light-weight covers. Too much man-made fabric is hot and clammy. Some mattresses have a thick man-made cover, and a cotton cover can make for a more comfortable sleep.

▶ Bed is for sleeping

You want your body to associate bed with relaxation and with sleeping. So for other activities, use a chair or sofa. If you have to sit on the bed, put a throw over it, and maybe some cushions. Wait until you're ready to go to sleep, before turning down the covers.

▶ Caffeine

Avoid caffeine in tea, coffee, drinks and foods such as chocolate during the evening. Caffeine is a stimulant and will keep you awake into the small hours. Try a hot milky drink, fruit juice, or fruit tea instead.

▶ Cigarettes

Cigarettes make it more difficult to get to sleep, and smokers wake more during the night, and have generally less deep restoring sleep.

▶ Alcohol

Alcohol can help you get to sleep, but after a few hours, its effects will disturb your sleep. It's also likely that you'll have to go to the toilet during the night too.

▶ Keep regular hours, even on weekends

Going to sleep and getting up at about the same time every day gives your body a programme to follow. Staying out late on weekends disrupts this.

▶ Exercise regularly – but not too close to bedtime

Take more exercise. Exercising during the day increases the time your body spends in deep sleep. But not within three hours of bedtime, as this will keep you awake.

▶ Busy mind

If your head is whirling with jobs to be done, or worries, it can help to make a list of each, along with what you'll do to sort each out the next day, then put this away. If that doesn't work, try any of the techniques for relaxing your mind from Chapter 6.

▶ Still awake?

If you still can't sleep, and have been wide awake for half an hour, don't continue tossing and turning, as this won't help. Better to get up and do something low-key and relaxing until you feel sleepy again. Then go back to bed.

▶ Wind down for bed

Just like babies and young children, winding down and relaxing for at least half an hour helps you to get to sleep. Your brain has to be ready for sleep, and this gives your brain waves and physiology a chance to settle down. Listen to some relaxing music or try some yoga or other relaxing activity before bedtime, as these will calm your body and brain (see Chapters 6, 11, or 13). Once in bed, you'll find any relaxation or breathing technique, or a mindfulness exercise from Chapters 5, 6 or elsewhere, which you've found works for you, will help you drift off to sleep. Sleep-style or abdominal breathing, covered in Chapter 5, can be particularly helpful when trying to sleep, or return to sleep.

Moving forward

If you haven't already, now is a good time to check back over all the ideas and techniques from this chapter, and note these in your Personal Journal (which you should have started earlier). Record anything which you felt would be helpful 'for now, for soon, or for a little further down the road'. There was a lot to take in all at once.

Focus points

1. Having a relaxed mind begins with a relaxed lifestyle.
2. To take your mind off something, you have to give your mind something else to think about, and to help your mind relax, you should give it something relaxing to think about.
3. There are many simple techniques for relaxing the mind including meditation, imagery, music, sounds, relaxing the muscles used for speech and sight.
4. To meditate you should have something to focus on: an object, picture, image or sound.
5. Having a regular good night's sleep is an important part of having a relaxed mind.

7

You can think yourself calm

In this chapter you'll discover how thinking can create stress. You'll learn how to reduce stress by changing your view of a situation, challenging irrational beliefs and adjusting your thinking so you think more positively. You'll also learn how being assertive can help you to manage stress.

'I change my thoughts, I change my world', was said by Norman Vincent Peale, author of the famous best seller, *The Power of Positive Thinking* some decades ago. It's hard to put it more clearly than that. And it remains true today. The last chapter was all about physical and practical techniques to calm and relax a tired and busy mind that just won't slow down. This chapter takes another approach to this entirely. Because the way we think is within our control, and we can change it. And stress, anxiety and worry are the products of our thinking, so we should be able to do something about that too. 'I change my thoughts, I change my world.' But how?

How do you feel?

Here are five key ideas from this chapter to think about now. They will be discussed later:

1 Which of these words or phrases do you use often? (Choose all that apply.)

   a Must

   b Awful

   c Ought

   d Horrendous

   e Should

   f Can't

   g Disastrous

2 Does the way you think make a big contribution to how stressed you are?

   a Don't know

   b Yes

   c No

   d Sometimes

   e Other

3 Do you ever...? (Choose all that apply.)

   a Jump to conclusions

   b Think life isn't fair

   c Want everyone to like you

   d Worry about making a mistake

   e None of these

4 How often would you say that you think in a negative way?

   a Never

   b Now and then

   c Frequently

   d All the time

   e Don't know

5 How are you behaving if you are being assertive? (Choose all that apply.)

   a Demanding what you want

   b Saying 'no'

   c Compromising

   d Sulking

   e Speaking up for yourself

   f Don't know

   g Looking after everybody's needs

Attacking stress on four fronts

We now come to the last of the four main groups of techniques for managing stress, *changing how we see a situation*. We have already explored the other three in some detail: *improve understanding, resolving the cause* and *cushioning*.

In Chapter 2, we divided stress management techniques into these four groupings, in an attempt to make such a broad subject simpler to track. But things are not always as simple as that. As you might expect, all stress management techniques are inter connected and inter related, and one will affect another. For example, having an explanation about how stress affects our mind and body will lower our stress levels, as it scares us less. This, in turn cushions us from its impact, and goes some way to resolving the cause, as part of the cause is the increased stress due to fear of what is happening to us. All of this together is of course going to change how we see the whole situation for the better.

In the same way, *changing how we see a situation* is helpful in itself, but it is also likely to provide a *cushioning* effect, and it may even wholly or partially *resolve the cause* of the stress itself, and go some way to *providing information and explanation too.*

Managing stress by changing our view of the world was introduced earlier in the book, and explained in broad terms in Chapter 6. This chapter will examine how you think, and what sorts of conversation go on with yourself in your head. And it will seek out any counter-productive habits you may have which can be changed to make you less stressed.

How thinking can create our stress

William Shakespeare said that 'There is nothing either good or bad, but thinking makes it so.' And we have already established that some people are able to think in a way which lets them remain positive and unbowed in the face of difficult circumstances, whilst others simply crumple and give up hope. The difference lies purely in how these individuals think about their situation. The difference is in their attitude to life – how they think about it.

Most of us fit in somewhere between these two extremes. Where do you think you might fit in? So what to do? What gives us a way forward is that our thinking is not fixed for life. It can be changed. Changing how you think won't take away the pain of a bereavement or serious illness, but we have already explored the greyer areas of stress, where whether or not we judge a situation to be a problem for us will decide if we feel stressed or not. This chapter is all about changing your thinking in ways which will mean you'll see fewer situations as a problem.

So how you think can affect you in *two* separate ways:

1 It decides how you are going to react to a stressful situation – be overwhelmed by it, or take it in your stride, or somewhere in between. Stress is not just about the situations we find ourselves in – it's about our reaction to that situation.

2 It can actually be the *cause of the feeling of stress in the first place*. Common examples of this would be expecting too much of ourselves, or expecting too much of other people.

So these two can combine to amplify their effect. We are not talking here about the kind of thinking which could be considered wrong or an illness. No, this is just normal everyday patterns and habits of thought and belief which can encourage and exacerbate stress in this modern world we find ourselves in. In a different place and time, they may not be a problem.

Remember this

We develop our thinking habits in childhood and in response to our experiences in life. These habits are also likely to be significantly affected by our cultural background.

REDUCE STRESS BY CHANGING THINKING

Theories of this kind first came on the scene around the 1960s and their success has prompted further developments. There are now many ways to alter thinking in a way that can reduce stress. Most importantly, you need to become aware of the thinking styles and beliefs which may be causing a problem. Then you have to put in place suggestions on how these might be changed. Many people find that simply becoming aware of their unhelpful thinking, along with their effects can be enough to yield a substantial, effective and long-lasting change.

To anyone not familiar with such techniques, they may seem somewhat unusual and off the wall. But they work, and they have been shown to work in numerous studies. Let's begin by looking at 'irrational' beliefs, and it will be easier to see what all the fuss is about. You'll also find how to challenge these in a way which reduces their effects.

CHALLENGING IRRATIONAL BELIEFS

One of the people to begin talking about 'irrational beliefs' was Dr Albert Ellis. In 1962, he described how stress can be the outcome of our beliefs about the world. He called these beliefs 'irrational' in the sense that they are very fixed and dogmatic views on the world, but when looked at closely, are unlikely to be the truth. These beliefs don't mean someone is ill in any way. Such beliefs are extremely common and entirely 'normal'. But they can cause stress and anxiety.

Here are a just a few of Dr Ellis's 'irrational beliefs' taken from an extensive list. It's easy to see how holding one of these beliefs very strongly can make life stressful even in the absence of a major stressor:

▶ I should be good at everything.

▶ I need everyone's approval for everything I do.

▶ I should not make a mistake.

▶ Life should be fair to me.

Most of these beliefs are opinions we come to hold as we grow up. Especially if achievement and success are highly prized by those around us. And even more so if praise is in short supply, but criticism of mistakes is never far away. Together, these circumstances, which have been particularly common over past decades, make up a fantastic recipe for low self-esteem and fear of failure for many people growing up in that sort of environment.

And these feelings of low self-esteem bring with them many of the above beliefs – I ought to be good at everything, I crave approval all the time, and I'm a failure if I make a mistake, or don't do well in everything. Put that way, it's easy to see the irrationality, but few of us can't identify at least a little with some of these beliefs. If someone can become aware, understand, challenge and then *change* such beliefs, their capacity for stress should be reduced.

So irrational beliefs are not undisputed truth, but have their roots in childhood and the culture around us. To remove their ability to cause stress, people should be encouraged to ask themselves where these beliefs are written down or stated. Here are three irrational or mistaken beliefs, along with ways of challenging them.

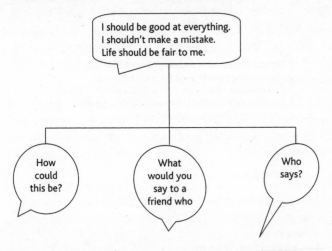

Many common stress-inducing beliefs and inner dialogues include the words 'ought', 'should' or 'must'. Here are some examples. For this kind of self-imposed expectation, and overly strict personal rules, you can challenge them by asking yourself, 'why?' and 'who says'?

▶ I should have done that by now. (Why? Who says?)

▶ I ought to phone him today. (Why? Who says?)

▶ I should tidy that cupboard. (Why? Who says?)

▶ I must not get this wrong. (Why? Who says?)

▶ I should have done that better/quicker/sooner. (Why? Who says?)

EXAGGERATING WITHOUT REALIZING IT

Other unhelpful beliefs and thoughts exaggerate the true reality of a situation, and are extremely common. We hear them every day in the street, or on buses and trains. These typically include words and phrases such as, 'awful', 'terrible' or 'I can't stand it'. *The weather is always absolutely dreadful, and the queues at the bank are horrendous.*

As before, challenging the belief can normalize it. Is the train delay really a 'disaster', or would 'inconvenient' be nearer the mark? Was your appraisal 'your worst nightmare', or would 'quite uncomfortable at times' be more like it? When you say 'I can't stand this', is it really as bad as that?

> Oh my god, you'll never believe the terrible time I had getting to work today! It was truly awful. A horrendous traffic jam. And just look at my in-tray. An absolutely enormous back-log to get through. It will take me forever to get through it!

There are two ways this 'exaggerating' causes problems. Firstly, what words and descriptions will you use if things get worse? But mainly, if you talk like this, you can almost feel the stress springing from you.

Case study

Esther is 32, and has gone to see her doctor because she's been feeling a bit down, and is stressed a lot of the time. She can't understand this as she has a job, which she enjoys, and she and partner Li have been together for eight years, and get on really well. Her GP asks her to describe her typical day, and she says, 'I get up, have a quick shower, and then have some coffee. I know I *should* eat breakfast, but I *have to* get the washing in the machine, and do a quick hoover round, so we can come back to a tidy flat. Then into that *useless* car of mine to drive to work. It's so *erratic*, and the traffic is *diabolical*. Morning at work is always *horribly* busy with clients, and flies past. I *must* pick up the shopping at lunchtime, as I usually finish late as I *have* to get everything done properly at work. Don't want to make any mistakes! Then I *have* to get home to cook dinner. I really *ought* to do more home cooking and making cupcakes and stuff, but trying to fit everything in is just *impossible. It isn't fair* really, I try so hard, but *I never seem to get it right*. There must be some easy answer to it all, because *everybody else seems to cope better than I do.'*

Much of Esther's thinking is causing her unnecessary stress. You can hear from her use of words like 'have to', 'ought' and 'must' that she sets rules and expectations for herself which are impossible to meet. She's staying late at work to make sure she has got everything right in what sounds like a busy job. She also exaggerates situations, like her 'useless' car, and the 'diabolical' traffic, and is angry with life because it doesn't all work out the way she wants.

It is quite common for much of this type of exaggerated and negative thinking to interlock together in this kind of 'ideology of life'. It's almost become a language itself, which you can hear being used on buses, or social network sites.

It's not that Esther deliberately thinks in this way. These are thinking habits and beliefs which can easily creep up on people in today's non-stop hectic world where success and coping are so valued, and everyone has so many plates spinning at the one time. Thinking in this way is often picked up from those around us.

THINKING MORE POSITIVELY

Over a lifetime of research, Dr Donald Meichenbaum, from Ontario in Canada, developed stress management techniques based on the idea that the constant inner conversation we have with ourselves, called self-speech, or self-talk, has a considerable effect on our behaviour. For example, it's very common to have a very negative and self-defeating style of self-speech. It's a kind of self-fulfilling prophecy, which builds on itself, reducing self-esteem and self-confidence more and more. This 'negative thinking' would include the well-known 'glass half empty rather than half full', and other thoughts such as:

- I always get things wrong.
- I can't do this.
- Things never work out for me.
- I don't think I can cope with it.
- This is too difficult for me.
- I'll never do this.
- I'm hopeless at this.

Oh, no. Here we go again!

The key idea here is that this kind of thinking is a habit, and one which can be changed. Like before, the first step is to begin to notice it, and the second is to use other, more positive phrases such as:

- I've coped with this before, so I can do it again.

I know I can do this if I try.

- Good enough is good enough.
- If it's difficult for me, it will be difficult for most people.
- I don't always get things wrong.
- I know I can do this quite well, and that will be good enough.

OTHER THINKING ERRORS

Our thinking is the product of many factors, not least how we happen to be feeling on a particular day. Whether we see the glass as half full or half empty, or believe that 'everyone should like me' is affected by our genes, the environment we were raised in, our education, and our life experience.

And the thinking habits and beliefs we acquire will inevitably contain some thinking errors. Here are some other common thinking errors which can contribute to feeling stressed. There is understandably some overlap and crossover amongst these.

Thinking error	How it will affect your behaviour
Black and white thinking	Very dogmatic, fixed thinking, with two distinct sides, and nothing in between. No shades of grey. Thinking of people and events in black and white, good or bad. So a friend who gets into debt 'has nobody to blame but themselves'.
Jumping to conclusions	A tendency to expect, and predict, that events or people will turn out badly, without considering more plausible explanations. For example, if someone's ten minutes late, something bad has happened to them, or they just don't want to see you.
Catastrophizing	Everything is out of proportion. Dwelling on the worst possible outcome of an event. If you miss a deadline at work, the whole project becomes a disaster in your mind.
Mental filter	Concentrating entirely on the negative aspects, as if the positive side didn't matter at all. You forget all the things which went well on a holiday, and let the fact the plane was delayed spoil and colour the entire holiday.
Overgeneralization	Believing that if something didn't work out once, it will never work out. So if a relationship ends badly, you think you might as well give up on finding a partner.
Personalization	Blaming yourself for anything negative that happens, with no reason. Whatever goes wrong or doesn't work out, you'll find something you did to cause this.

How to de-stress your thinking

The first and most important thing to do if you want to stress-proof your thinking is to become aware of how your everyday thoughts and beliefs can impact on your life experience. This can be a real revelation to most people. And if you've read this chapter to here, you've already taken that important first step.

The second thing to do is to learn how to 'challenge' or 'question' these thoughts whenever they occur. To do this, there are several questions you can ask yourself about the problem thought which can really take away most of the stress it's causing.

HOW TO CHALLENGE UNHELPFUL THOUGHTS AND BELIEFS

Whenever you find yourself with 'unhelpful' thoughts or beliefs going through your mind, which make you feel worried, stressed, anxious, or tense, ask yourself these eight questions, think them through, and answer them honestly.

- What is the evidence supporting this thought?

- Who says it's true?

- Is it written down somewhere that this is true?

- What are the chances of it being true?

- Is there an alternative 'helpful' explanation/s?

- What is the evidence supporting the alternative explanation/s?

- What would I tell a friend if he or she were in the same situation?

- Is there a more realistic and positive thought?

You may also find it useful to give a rating of 0–100 for how much you believe the unhelpful thought before questioning it, and again afterwards, and see if you can make a difference.

It also helps to keep a note of your answers in this process, so you can remind yourself of these, if the thought comes back.

THOUGHT STOPPING

When you just can't get a thought out of your mind, 'thought stopping' can be a useful technique. What you do is keep thinking (or saying out loud) the word 'STOP!' emphatically, over and over until your mind goes onto something else. This takes practice, and it can take a few repeats, but it can really help. Try it out first when you don't really need it. You'll get better at it the more you do it. You can use any word or phrase for this which suits you, and even include 'expletives' in certain circumstances. Examples are:

- STOP

- CALM MY MIND

- LEAVE MY MIND

- GO AWAY NOW

- I DON'T WANT YOU IN MY MIND

- DISAPPEAR NOW.

ATTENTION SWITCHING

This is all about trying to move the mind away from what's troubling it. You do this by occupying your mind with a mental activity which requires concentration. This will switch your attention away from your unwanted thinking. Some ideas:

► Count backwards from 200 in sevens.

> 200, 193, 186, 179,

► List the prime numbers, or multiples of six or eight from 0. Repeat a times table.

► Try to think of a boy's or girl's name for every letter of the alphabet. Or an animal, or a food or whatever.

► Learn and recite a poem, a song or a piece from Shakespeare. Don't try anything too difficult. The main idea is to distract your thoughts.

► In a crowded room or in town, count the number of people wearing a particular colour, then move on to another colour, and so on.

► If you're on a bus, or a passenger in a car, focus on car number plates, and see if you can make a word out of all of the letters. Try to work out the make of every car you see.

FINDING REPLACEMENT NEUTRAL THOUGHTS

Make up a table like the one below, in your notebook.

Over the next few days and weeks, look out for any 'unhelpful thoughts' you have, and carry a small sticky note pad with you to jot these down, then stick them into your notebook later on.

When you have time, have a try at working out an alternative 'neutral' thought for each one – you're looking for a more objective, positive and realistic thought.

There's a few here to start you off, and show you the idea. The more you practise doing this, the less unhelpful thoughts you'll have.

Unhelpful thought	Alternative neutral thought/s
She always lets me down	She gets things wrong sometimes, but most of the time she's great. She tries really hard, but her father has been ill, and it's affecting her concentration.
He is looking at me as if I'm stupid.	He is looking, but he could be thinking anything. He may be worrying about his job. He may not have his contacts in.
She doesn't care about me.	She forgot this time, but she is usually very loving, so she does care. The baby has been keeping her up at night, so she's very tired.

Assertiveness

Remember the four categories of stress management techniques introduced earlier? You are probably quite familiar with these now:

▶ Learn more about stress

▶ Remove or reduce the cause or causes

▶ Cushioning from the effects of the stress

▶ Changing how you see the situation.

It's time to introduce a topic which may have some relevance in terms of removing or reducing the cause of your stress. Sometimes stress is caused by not being assertive enough. Improving your assertiveness skills may help you cope better with situations at work, and in dealing with friends, neighbours and loved ones.

As already mentioned, there is some cross-over amongst the four categories. Assertiveness is one technique which tends to fit into two categories – it can both help to *resolve the cause* of a person's stress, but it can also have a role in *cushioning*.

HOW ASSERTIVE ARE YOU?
Rate whether you agree or disagree with each statement on a scale of 1–7, and enter the number in Column 3, or in your notebook.

1 = strongly agree

2 = moderately agree

3 = slightly agree

4 = neither agree nor disagree

5 = slightly disagree

6 = moderately disagree

7 = strongly disagree

Statement	Column 1	Column2	Your score
I tend to put my needs last			
I like to get what I want no matter what			
I have difficulty saying 'no' to people			
I often give in to other people's wishes and set aside my own			
I find being criticized difficult			
I am prone to aggressive outbursts			
I feel much better about myself if I please other people			
I find it difficult to say what I really think			
I often think other people are more important than I am			
I don't like to compromise			
I find it difficult to return things to a shop			
I don't like to be the centre of attention			
I say 'I'm sorry' a lot			
I often get my way be making others feel guilty			
I find speaking up in a group difficult			
TOTAL SCORE			

Now total up your score, to give a general indication of your assertiveness rating.

As a very rough guide, scores over 85 indicate you are almost always assertive, 70–84, you are assertive most of the time, 40–69 assertive some of the time, 20–39 only assertive occasionally, 0–19 hardly ever or never assertive.

Low levels of assertiveness usually indicate a great deal of passive behaviour, such as not being able to say 'no' to people, and generally being the dogsbody. This is often linked to a lack of confidence and low self-esteem, which is often due to childhood or previous life experiences. Low levels can also indicate a tendency to dominate others, or sometimes be aggressive, sulky or manipulative.

Now choose two people you know well, maybe a friend and a colleague or manager from work – don't write down their names – and repeat the questionnaire rating them in your view, for each statement, in Columns 1 and 2, or in your notebook. Total these up. Has this turned up any surprises? Or confirmed what you already thought? It's not just whether you yourself are assertive which may be relevant here; it's also to do with how assertive the people you deal with every day are. Having to deal with people who are not assertive can also be very stressful.

WHAT DOES ASSERTIVENESS HAVE TO DO WITH STRESS?*
Stressful situations often arise from people not being able to communicate their needs and wishes to others, either at work or in relationships, or both. And assertiveness is all about just that – being able to express what you feel or what you want in a calm, confident yet non-threatening way. Everyone's behaviour will vary from situation to situation, but if a lot of what we do is not assertive, this can cause stress.

Here are some people who are not behaving assertively, and who are likely to generate stress for themselves, or create stress in others who have to deal with them. Do you recognize yourself or others you come into contact with in this list?

People who:

- don't listen to your point of view or what you have to say
- find they can never say 'no'
- cannot speak up about their own needs to others
- are rude or aggressive to others
- tend to dominate or control other people
- get their own way by making others feel guilty
- cannot give criticism without devaluing the other person
- have to win at all costs
- can't make up their minds
- use sarcasm
- can't compromise.

WHAT EXACTLY IS ASSERTIVENESS?

Assertiveness is based on the idea that everyone is equal, has the same rights and that we should all have respect for ourselves and other people. We should all be able to communicate on a level playing field, in other words. Assertiveness is often confused with aggression, but aggression is the direct opposite, as we'll see later.

If you behave assertively, you:

- know your own needs
- are aware of your own strengths and weaknesses
- have genuine respect for yourself
- have genuine respect for others
- are open, direct and honest whenever appropriate
- know how to compromise.

Mythbuster

Being assertive doesn't mean being aggressive, pushy and overbearing. It is the opposite. Assertiveness is about treating yourself and others with respect.

NON-ASSERTIVE BEHAVIOUR

If you aren't behaving assertively, you are likely to conduct yourself in one of these alternative ways:

▶ **Aggressive**

Angry, in your face, verbally abusive, threatening, domineering, competitive, dogmatic, must have own way, must win, must be right....

▶ **Manipulative (also called 'indirect aggression')**

Getting your own way by making others feel guilty, by sulking, by sarcasm and put-downs....

▶ **Over-confident**

Nothing is a problem, loud, you know best, full of ideas, you know everything, one-upmanship, you know everyone....

▶ **Passive**

No confidence, dropping hints, making excuses, unable to say 'no', the dogsbody, difficulty making decisions, apologizing all the time, putting everyone else first all the time....

▶ **Passive-aggressive**

Behaving passively most of the time, and then flipping over into aggression every so often as frustration builds up – 'the worm turning'.

Recognize yourself in some or all of these descriptions? Remember our behaviour varies from situation to situation. You might be manipulative with your partner, passive at work, and aggressive with door-to-door sales-people. Or you might just be having one of those days.

All of this behaviour could be placed along a line, or a continuum, with assertiveness in the centre, and aggressive and passive at either end.

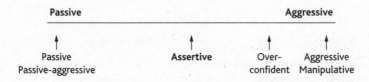

Passive		Aggressive
↑	↑	↑ ↑
Passive	Assertive	Over- Aggressive
Passive-aggressive		confident Manipulative

HOW TO BE MORE ASSERTIVE

Here are some suggestions for becoming more assertive more of the time, if you think that would be useful, but remember to take this slowly and gradually, and try out one new thing at a time. If you find these ideas particularly helpful, you could think about enrolling for a full course, or read up more on the subject.

Tick or underline or make a note of any of these you might find helpful:

General:

▶ value *yourself*

▶ value *other people*

▶ work out *your* priorities in life: choose them for *yourself*

▶ work out what you *need* and *want* in life

▶ be prepared to compromise

▶ keep to any point you're making – don't let others distract you from it

▶ speak with a warm, steady and low-pitched voice

▶ keep your head up, use regular eye contact and confident posture

▶ get your feeling of self-worth from within yourself, not just from other people

▶ never act aggressively, or threaten people

▶ have confidence in yourself, and don't be timid

- don't look for proof of your value as a person from others through your obliging ways – get your feeling of self-worth from within yourself, and get to like yourself – remember nobody's perfect, neither you nor other people!

Saying 'No':

- keep it short, and say it confidently but warmly
- only give a reason if you want to
- only apologize if you feel it's right to do so
- use a simple phrase you're comfortable with, such as 'I don't want to' or 'I'd rather not'.

Practise saying the words out loud, so that you're comfortable with them and calmly repeat your 'No' if the first one is not accepted.

Never forget you have these rights:

- to make a mistake
- to have your own point of view
- to fail if you try something
- to expect others to listen to you
- to feel anxious at first.

Deal with your anger

You can't be assertive if you're angry. So, if you're angry, take time out to use breathing or relaxation exercises to calm yourself.

Taking up a contact sport such as football or judo, or going for a jog or a cycle, or cleaning the windows can be a great release.

EASY DOES IT

You may have no problems with assertiveness – not everyone does. But what can you do if you feel you're not assertive enough, often enough, or there are some situations which need improvement? This can take time to change as you are learning new skills, and often trying to break the habits of a lifetime.

If you're going to try out any of these assertiveness techniques, remember:

▶ Don't jump in with both feet. Think it through first.

▶ Put any new behaviour or techniques into practice slowly and carefully.

▶ Start with 'easy' situations to develop your confidence, then work slowly towards more difficult situations, building your confidence as you go.

▶ Don't feel pressure to make big changes…it's all up to you.

Remember this

Assertiveness is not about being aggressive, it is simply about being able to express your needs and views in a calm effective manner in a way which respects both you and the other person/s involved. Sometimes all you need is the confidence in yourself.

Relaxing the mind and body in the long term

Your progress will vary across the many techniques for managing stress you've been introduced to so far in Chapters 5, 6 and 7. Be assured there is no race or competition to see how quickly you can learn these skills, or how well you can manage your stress. The main aim is for you to progress at the rate that is right for you. If stress has been a big problem for you for a long time, progress may be a bit slower than if stress has only become a challenge recently.

So what to do at this stage is simply to continue practising the new skills you've selected to the level you are happy with, and move on whenever you feel the time is right to do so. Use your Personal Journal and your notes to stay on track. All this will also *improve your sense of being in a control.*

Control is a theme which has run through much of the discussion of stress thus far. We saw how people vary in the extent to which they feel they can affect their situation, and have some control over what happens to them. Those with what was described as an 'external locus of control' feel they have very little control, and may be appraising their situation wrongly, and have taken none of the available steps to reduce their stress.

Stress management is above all else about empowering people and enabling them to deal with their difficulties effectively. There are many situations over which people really do have little control, and in such circumstances, building resilience and cushioning is the way forward for them.

This idea may explain the difference between people who are crushed and those who flourish when faced with adversity. The former sees the situation as beyond their control and gives up, whilst the latter takes control and puts into place the required action to build their resilience and turn the situation around.

SOME MORE HINTS AND TIPS FOR HEALTHY THINKING

▶ Don't ignore the positive or ordinary things that happen each day, as if they don't count for some reason. Take account of the negatives, but *don't define your day by them, and don't dwell on them*. Put something positive into your mind instead.

▶ Take your mind *off* your problems as much as you can – they grow bigger the more you concentrate on them – but shrink into proportion when you think about something else.

▶ Remember problems and mistakes are not always *your* fault – other people, chance, or just the situation are more likely to be the cause.

▶ Try thinking a *positive* thought *frequently* throughout the day – 'what a lovely smile that man has', or 'I love the colour of that coat'. *Your* thoughts are up to you, *but keep them coming!* It may sound trivial, but it really works....

- When discouraging and negative thoughts pop into your mind like, 'I can't do this', 'I'll never get that job', *challenge* these thoughts. What evidence is there to support these thoughts – and what about the evidence against them? How would others view the situation? What would you say to a friend who felt that way?

- Get to know who you are, and like what you find. There will never be anyone else quite the same as *you*.

- Lots of people, despite how they appear, are often as unsure of themselves as you are.

- Don't let yourself be drawn into 'negative' conversation, texts, social network site discussion, or e-mails. Change the subject to something more positive.

- Go for friends who have positive thinking habits.

- You can't carry the entire world around on *your* shoulders. Give someone else a share!

- Practise *liking* people.

- Count your blessings – an old idea, but still true! Every night before you go to sleep, think of three good things you have.

Focus points

1. Get the most from relaxation by practising every day with your choice of:

   * relaxation technique to relax your body
   * relaxation technique to relax your mind
   * breathing technique.

2. When ready, begin to use any of these techniques in your everyday life too, whenever they can help you feel less stressed.

3. How you think can create stress for yourself, but you can change this.

4. Being more assertive, more often, can defuse many stressful situations, and make them manageable.

5. There are many ways you can think more 'healthily', which can boost self-confidence, and reduce stress.

8

Coping with panic attacks

A very frightening outcome of stress is the panic attack, sometimes called an anxiety attack. It is called an attack because it seems to come on strongly and without any reason, sometimes out of a blue sky, and it leaves again just as unpredictably. Or at least that's how it seems. In this chapter, you'll find out that a panic attack is much more predictable than it seems. And that makes it easier to deal with.

How do you feel?

Here are five key ideas from this chapter to think about now. They will be discussed later:

1 Do you ever suddenly feel acutely anxious, panicky, afraid, or stressed, but the feelings subside again within 20 minutes to half an hour?

2 If so, how often does this happen? What do you do?

3 Have you heard of a panic or anxiety attack?

4 Do you notice any other symptoms in your body or mind?

5 Do you know anyone who has panic attacks? A friend? A member of the family?

Not everyone who is stressed will experience panic. And not everyone who has a panic attack is stressed. For many people, a panic attack can happen just once out of the blue, and never again. Or these attacks can be part of a broader pattern. But as we saw in Chapter 1, panic attacks or a general feeling of low-grade panic or fear is a very common outcome of stress.

America's Institute of Health currently estimates that 6 million Americans experience repeated panic attacks. They also suggest that twice as many women as men are affected, and that the tendency towards panic attacks is inherited in most cases. In the UK, the NHS Choices website estimates that in 2012 one person in ten in the UK experiences occasional panic attacks, usually as an outcome of stress.

Panic attacks typically begin fairly suddenly, and often from nowhere, with a sharp increase in anxiety, which usually peaks within ten minutes, and then slowly subsides. An attack can last from 5–30 minutes. Your stomach may churn, heart race, breathing may be rapid, and you may sweat, feel faint, feel overwhelming fear and panic, and a sense of impending disaster, along with a pressing need to escape from the situation you find yourself in. Some people find themselves rooted to the spot. No matter how the panic attack affects you, it is a distressing and very frightening way to feel.

As we discussed already in Chapter 1, panic attacks are a form of particularly acute but short-lasting anxiety, and are the body's normal reaction to *physical* danger. They are really the body's 'fight or flight' reaction which happens completely automatically when we are in physical danger, allowing us increased supplies of energy and muscle tone to help us to either run away from or fight whatever is endangering us. Clearly this is a very primitive, but essential part of us. If we had to take the time to work out what to do when a speeding car suddenly bears down on us whilst crossing the street, it would already be too late. The 'fight or flight' reaction does it for us before we have time to think. This accounts for how it feels: fear, a feeling that something awful is going to happen, racing heart, muscle tension, an almost irresistible need to leave where we are and go somewhere safer, such as our car or home.

So, a panic attack is the 'fight, flee or freeze' response happening in a body which isn't in physical danger at all. But why? Panic attacks are often triggered by events, or even by something as transient and unsubstantial as a fleeting thought, especially with a sensitized nervous system. 'What if I can't get this done in time?' 'What if I can't pay those bills?' 'What if' questions are a common source of anxiety.

Understanding what is happening and how to deal with it, can diffuse a situation which, if nothing is done about it, can surprisingly quickly produce avoidance behaviour which can lead to life-restricting phobias such as agoraphobia.

Case study

Mark walked hesitantly into his doctor's consulting room, looking pale and worried. He could hardly remember the last time he saw a doctor. Probably that strained muscle from an overly keen shot at squash two years ago. Mark is 36, married and a teacher. He avoided the female doctor's eyes, as he blurted out that he was sure he was losing his mind. Yesterday at work he had 'come over kind of strange'. He described how he couldn't think straight, was convinced something terrible was about to happen, and his heart had pounded. The weirdest thing was that he had also had a feeling of acute panic, and had found himself rushing out of the classroom without getting cover, and without even explaining to the class of 12-year-olds. The funny thing was that as soon as he got to the staffroom at the other end of the school, he felt fine again. What was happening to him, he asked, now looking straight at the doctor. Was this a nervous breakdown? What would everyone think? What if it should happen again? Gentle questioning by the doctor revealed that Mark had been under pressure for months as he and his wife Paloma were moving house, and had already bought a house, but couldn't sell their own. He wasn't sleeping well, and felt tired all the time.

A panic attack happening like this, at work, can be very frightening. It feels like being the victim of a terrifying attack over which you appear to have absolutely no control. You can be convinced they you going mad or are about to die. But it can all be over in a matter of minutes, as if it had never happened.

If you don't regain control over these attacks which seem to strike out of the blue, a vicious circle can establish itself. As you've no idea what caused it, you worry about the next attack, and perhaps begin to avoid the situations which you fear may provoke another attack. The fleeting thought, 'What if I panic now?', can immediately set off the feared attack. It's important to do something about the problem straight away. So, what can you do if you have panic attack?

Four steps to controlling panic attacks*

Just as stress is best tackled on the four fronts mentioned earlier (learn more about stress, remove/reduce cause, cushioning and resilience, and seeing the problem differently), panic attacks are best tackled in this way too. So, there are four steps to controlling panic:

Step one: as described already, your level of stress is often substantially reduced simply by understanding the bodily processes which makes you feel the way you do. This is even truer for panic attacks. Once the 'fight or flight' reaction has been explained and understood, the fantasy of an unpredictable and terrifying attack can be transformed into the reality of a completely natural automatic defence mechanism as we've described already in Chapters 1 and 2. This can have a rapid and remarkable effect, and I hope these chapters have been helpful in this way. If you've been dipping into the book, and have not read that section yet, go back now and have a look.

Step two: reduce stress levels as much as you can, by removing or reducing the cause of the stress if possible.

Step three: build your resilience, and cushion yourself from your stressors as much as possible using the range of the techniques covered so far in this book. These strategies will help to soothe and desensitize your nervous system, and make the panic attack much less likely to recur. Your nervous system can become very sensitive, a bit like a loose trigger, or a tall column of children's blocks just ready to topple when the next small brick is added. Regular relaxation calms your nervous system, making it much less likely to fire off.

Step four: You have to see the problem in a different way. To do this, start two new pages in your notebook, and have some sticky note pads handy. Place a heading in the centre of the top of the first page, 'Signs of a panic attack', and on the second, 'What was happening, or what was I thinking just before the panic attack?' Keep at least one sticky note pad in your pocket, or preferably two different shapes or colours, so that you can write down your feelings, and bodily sensations just before the attack on the one, and what was going on around you, or inside your head, on the other.

The PAUSE Routine

You are now all set to do something about your panic attacks. Franklin Roosevelt, former President of the United State of America, once famously said, 'We have nothing to fear but fear itself'. Learning what a panic attack is, that it will do you no harm, and that you should be able to take control of it yourself, will therefore help to mitigate their effects, and even make them less likely to happen in the first place.

As the panic response is an automatic process, like breathing, simply telling your body not to panic will not be effective. Do you remember we covered that in Chapter 1? Physical relaxation techniques on the other hand, can reach behind the automatic response, allowing the brain to realize that the danger is subsiding, and begin to press the 'no need to panic button'. The PAUSE routine, which we'll explain shortly, describes clearly how to do this.

If you have panic attacks, the key is to catch them in their early stages, and stop them there. Be on the alert for the first signs of a panic attack beginning (you should have worked that out in the previous activity). Then, you should use a quick relaxation or breathing technique straight away, as this will inhibit and possibly prevent the panic attack progressing any further.

This also puts you back in control. You probably feel as if the panic just flashes instantaneously, without warning, but if you have followed step three above, you should have noticed a few warning signs, like a lurch in your stomach, or your heart rate beginning to rise.

Here is one way of doing this. When you panic, it's hard to think straight, and remember what to do. That's why I created the PAUSE routine, to make it easier during a panic attack to know what to do. Don't be put off if this method doesn't work the first or even second time you try it. Keep at it. It takes a bit of practice for some people, and a bit of determination, but it is very effective. Thousands of people have used it successfully. You can too.

 Try it now

Pause routine

If you have a panic attack, or begin to feel panicky, the trick is to catch this early, and stop it there. This puts you back in control. Here is one way of doing this.

Work out what are your own first signs of a panic attack. This might be a lurch in the stomach, a thought in your mind, heart rate rising, or something else you've noticed.

Look out for these first signs, and when you notice them, you should immediately:

Pause...and make yourself comfortable (sit down, lean on something, etc.)

Absorb...detail of what's going on around you

Use...any method of relaxing quickly which works well for you, *then*

Slowly....when you feel better,

Ease...yourself back into what you were doing.

This is where all that practising and learning quick ways of relaxing pays off. When using the PAUSE routine, you can use whichever of these methods has worked best for you – be it any of the types of Rapid Relaxation, or a breathing technique. This is when it will come into its own.

Focus points

1. Panic or anxiety attacks are very common, especially for women, and are often brought on by stress.
2. They are caused by the body's 'fight, freeze or flight' reaction from the ANS, which believes the body is threatened in some way.
3. They seem to come out the blue, but you'll have had a fleeting thought, or seen or heard something which reminds you of something relevant.
4. Knowing your first sign of a panic attack helps you to deal with it before it has properly begun, using the PAUSE routine.
5. Using any relaxation technique which works for you. This will dampen down the fight or flight process before it's had time to get started. This is the only language the ANS understands.

9

The gentle power of mindfulness

This chapter explores the concept of mindfulness, a powerful tool in managing stress. You'll learn how to be mindful, which is all about living in the present moment, and how this can help you to combat stress and panic.

Mindfulness

Mindfulness is a relative newcomer to the world of stress management, but it is one of the most powerful and effective techniques to have come into common use in recent years. However, it isn't a new invention, it's a skill that human beings have used for many centuries, in a number of different guises. Mindfulness, or being mindful, is all about being aware of the present moment, paying close attention to it, and experiencing it to the full.

It has had close connections with the Buddhist faith for thousands of years, but it doesn't have to be associated with a particular belief system. It's simply been used over the centuries by many belief systems as a way of encouraging people to clear their minds of other things, and focus without distraction. Any type of prayer uses the same skill. In the past few decades, the importance of mindfulness for managing stress has been realized.

Mythbuster

Mindfulness is not a belief system or a religion, and you don't have to be religious to use it. It is one our most ancient and basic human skills, and it can be used easily and successfully, completely separately from any religious links at all.

How do you feel?

Here are five key ideas from this chapter to think about now. They will be discussed later:

1 Estimate how much of your day you spend with your mind:

   a In the past (recent or otherwise)

   b In the present, or the here and now

   c Thinking ahead (near or distant future).

2 In your general everyday life, which of these do you do regularly (choose all that apply)?

  a Think very quickly

  b Think very slowly

  c Feel as if you're in the here and now

  d Have lots of thoughts on your mind at the same time

  e Judge yourself and others

  f Concentrate only on one thing.

3 In what ways would your answers to question two have been different:

  a One year ago?

  b Five years ago?

  c Ten years ago?

  d When you were aged around ten?

4 When did you last notice yourself breathing?

5 Put your hands over your ears so you can't hear. Now...what do you expect to hear when you take your hands away? Now take your hands away, and really listen. Do you hear more or less than you expected?

Notice the moment

With the busy lives most of us lead, it's very easy to have your mind on the day or week's schedule ahead, and never quite notice the moment you're actually living in. And that's where our life is lived, in the moment. For some people, their thoughts are constantly on days that have past: opportunities missed, loved ones now gone, mistakes made, hurts given and received. So much so, that they miss the moment, they miss the here and now, where we all live.

When you are mindful, you bring your mind from the past or from the future into the here and now, into the moment. And you closely observe that moment in which you find yourself. You pay close attention to your thoughts, feelings and sensations, but you don't judge, react or reflect on these.

If you pay attention closely to one thing, in the moment, you are being mindful. Staring at the waves crashing over the rocks onto the beach, and thinking of nothing else, is being mindful. Watching a bee flit from flower to flower, hearing its buzzing sound increase as it enters the flower, with nothing else on your mind, is being mindful. Even watching the traffic endlessly flow past you in the city centre as you wait for your bus, and listening to the changing sound, without any other distractions, is mindfulness.

Try it now

Mindful breathing

Sit down in a comfortable chair, read what you've to do first, then gently close your eyes. Now without really trying, bring your thoughts to your breathing. Become aware of your breathing, and the feeling of the air entering and leaving your body, as you breathe in and out. Notice the slight rise and fall of your chest. Continue in this way for two or three minutes, just concentrating on your breathing. If any other thoughts intrude, just notice them, don't be at all concerned about this, then return your thoughts to your breathing.

Being mindful is a skill we all have, but many of us have lost the habit and simply forgotten to use it, in this hurly burly existence we have today. It is similar to meditation, but is probably simpler and easier to learn, or more accurately, to refresh your memory about. It isn't just another way to relax. It's much more than that. It's a way of being too, which provides a very effective cushion from stress 24/7.

Remember this

In mindfulness, the here and now, the present moment is all that matters. Each breath is replaced effortlessly by the next breath. You exist with no other purpose than being alive, awake and aware of that moment.

So, mindfulness is all about maintaining a calm, non-judging awareness, and allowing thoughts, feelings, and sensations to just come and go without getting involved in them. It's a way of being. The past has gone, the future is yet to come, and what exists between them is the present moment, the here and now, which we often don't notice at all, a bit like the express train that speeds through a tiny country station without even slowing down to take in the view. Mindfulness is about living in the moment, enjoying it, and experiencing all its sensations fully, and without judgement. And it's really easy to do.

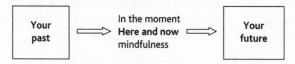

EXPERIENCE IT FOR YOURSELF

Start a new page in your Personal Journal and head it 'Mindfulness'. Carry some sticky notes or a small notepad and pencil around with you for the next few days. Whenever you have an opportunity, spend a few moments (or more if you can) being mindful in any way which seems right for you, which you read about in this chapter. Each occasion you're mindful, even for a few seconds, as soon as you've finished, use a new sticky note to make a note of the following to place in your notebook:

▶ what you did

▶ how well it worked on a 0 to 10 scale

▶ how it felt

▶ anything else you think worth noting.

How mindfulness can help stress

Mindfulness is a 'way of being', and this way of being can provide you with a long-lasting cushion and resilience from stress. So becoming more mindful in your everyday life is going to strengthen your armour for when there is a stressor to be coped with. Here is what underlies and creates this 'way of being', and how you can achieve it:

▶ Mindfulness is about the mind *and* the heart – so bring more kindness and compassion into your life.

▶ Move towards being less judgemental, less black and white in your thinking.

▶ Focus more on the 'here and now'.

- Move from knee-jerk reactions to a considered response.
- Focus your attention where it's needed.

Try it now

Simply mindful

Look around now wherever you are. Choose an object you find interesting, large or small, every day or unusual. Don't spend any time choosing, anything will do: a chair, book, cup, biscuit, curtain, rug, table, pen, whatever.

Now read what to do, and then make yourself comfortable, and try it for a minute or two.

What to do: When you've chosen the object, just bring yourself into the here and now, letting go any thoughts about what's happening later today or tomorrow, or happened earlier today, or in the past. Let these thoughts just drift away, and place all your attention on to your chosen object. With each outward breath, allow any remaining thoughts to go with your breath. Now look carefully at the object and take in everything about it: its shape, colour/s, size, texture of its surfaces, how the light falls on it, any shadows on it, and anything else you want to look for. It sounds a little strange, but you'll be surprised at how it makes you feel. When you feel you've finished, let your focus leave the object and begin to broaden and take in everything around you again.

Other ways you can live more mindfully

Mindfulness is a way of being, and it can also be a way of life. And this way of life is one which can provide an escape from the rat race, and a quiet and peaceful haven from a non-stop world. Here is a description of a mindful lifestyle.

- Try to just 'be' in the here and now, as much as you can. Use any opportunities in your day to do this, such as waiting for something or someone.

- In bed, feel the sensations of the duvet cover against your body, and your feet on the sheet. Notice the warmth the duvet creates.

- In the shower or bath, notice the fragrances, the sensation of the water and the towel on your skin, your bare feet on the bathroom floor.

- Pause before each meal. Eat more slowly and savour each mouthful. Enjoy your meals; focus on the textures, the flavours, the aroma, the colours. Feel the touch of the spoon on your hand.

- Avoid multi-tasking whenever you can.

- Become aware of your toes and feet in your shoes, the feeling of each foot as it makes contact with the floor, as you walk.

- Every day, wherever you go, notice colour, and notice texture.

- When out and about outside, pay attention to the sounds you hear, be that the traffic, or the leaves rustling in the park.

- Notice fragrances, and smells of all kinds, from the pleasant waft as someone walks past, to the appetizing smells as you pass the baker's shop.

- Be aware of the changing seasons, and how this shows itself in the garden, on the roads and railways, and in our surroundings, and our clothing.

- Notice people, their body language, expressions, clothing, voice, hair.

- At work, or recreation, focus and pay attention. If your mind wanders, don't be annoyed by it, just notice it, and gently return your thoughts.

- Carry out a mindfulness session every day – for at least five minutes. This can be whatever you like: focus on an object, a short walk, some music, washing the windows, or while jogging, running, cycling or on a bus or train.

MINDFULNESS AND TENSION

This is an example of how you can mindfully focus on your stress and the tension it causes in your muscles:

Take a few moments to sit down and make yourself comfortable. Slow down your body. Take in a long, slow, deep breath, hold it for a count of two, and then release it slowly, taking as long as you can to fully exhale. Then allow your breath to come and go in its own time, and notice the sensation of your breath entering and leaving your body.

Now it's time to notice your muscles. We are usually too busy and preoccupied with other things to notice what our muscles are doing. Think about them now…pay attention to your muscles…

Now, pay close attention to the muscles in your hands…your arms…your shoulders…your back…the back of your neck…. Are these muscles relaxed? Are they just right? Or do they feel too tense for what you're doing? If so, let the extra tension go with your next exhaled breath….

Then your face…and your forehead…and scalp. There can be so much tension here. Bring your attention to all these areas, and scan them now…around your eyes…around your mouth… are your teeth clenched?…your cheeks?…your nose?…your forehead? More tense than they need to be? Let any tension go with your next breath….

Now, one last check around all your muscles…release any remaining tension…and then become aware of the sensations you're now feeling all over your body. Spend a couple of minutes experiencing the relaxed feelings you've created.

Then slowly become more alert again, and more aware of your surroundings, until you're fully alert again.

Start from today noticing your muscles, and paying attention to them. Release any unnecessary tension, which you become aware of. Become much more self-aware. And you will become more relaxed, and more resilient to stress.

MINDFULNESS ON THE MOVE

You don't have to sit still to be mindful. If anything, it's easier on the move:

▶ Live in the moment. Experience every detail. Don't miss a thing.

▶ At home, feel the texture of each item as you load up the washing machine. Notice the sound of the water running into the kettle, and the click as you switch it on. Hear the quiet roar of the burning gas against the bottom of the pan as you cook dinner.

▶ At work, feel the sensation as each finger touches the keyboard, your hand on the mouse, your feelings, your voice, and your breathing as you chat to colleagues at lunchtime. As you travel home on the train, notice each feeling, each reaction to those around you, and notice the world passing by the window. Trees, people's back gardens, life going on inside many windows.

▶ Notice your touch on the front door handle as you arrive home, and on your key as you turn it in the lock.

▶ Feel the warmth of the washing-up water as you do the washing-up. Focus on the gestures, the facial expressions, and the stories of the friend you drop round to see. Then as you drive home again, see the textures and colours of the late evening sky.

MINDFULNESS AND WALKING

When you're out and about walking, wherever that is, from the park, to quiet woodland, the beach, or the city and the shops, here is how you can do this mindfully, even if it's just for a few minutes of your walking time:

▶ Just be in the moment, wherever you are. Put your destination to the back of your mind for a few moments.

▶ Don't walk too fast, so that you can pay attention to your body moving. Focus in turn on the movement and sensations of your head, body, each arm, each leg, each foot and your toes.

▶ Notice your legs and feet, as you lift each foot and place it back on the ground, and what that feels like in the sole of your foot. How does it sound? Is it wet or muddy, or dry underfoot? What are your toes doing? Can you feel them inside your shoes?

▶ What are your arms doing? Swinging to the rhythm of your walking, or close by your side, or holding a bag, or hands in pockets, or maybe fingers cosy inside gloves? Feel your fingers touching the inside of the glove, or the inside of your pocket, or grasping the textured strap of a bag, or a dog lead.

▶ What can you hear? Are there any fragrances or smells? What can you see close by?

▶ What does the breeze on your hair or your ears feel like? Is it cold or warm? Are you wearing a hat or a scarf? Can you feel the texture and warmth of the fabric against your skin?

Case study

Erik, age 41, has a partner and daughter, age 10.

Erik was finding his work very stressful. He is a telecommunications engineer, a role which he enjoyed, but his role had recently changed, and he had to do much more travelling now, and he missed his family and friends at home when he was away. He was beginning to think he'd have to change his job, as the stress and tension when he was away was becoming unbearable. A magazine he picked up for something to read at the dentist changed things for him. There was an article on mindful walking, so he gave it a try in the evenings, the next time he was away from home. He found it fascinating, and he found that he felt much better after having a mindful walk for a few evenings after work.

MINDFULNESS AND BREATHING

At any point in your day, simply concentrate on your breathing. Take each breath in through your nose and out through your mouth, and pay attention to allowing your tummy to swell up more than your chest. Be totally aware of the sound, the movement, the sensations in your nose, your mouth, your lungs. In the moment, really feel the rhythm of your breathing.

MINDFULNESS, MUSIC AND SOUNDS

Choose any music or recorded sound which is calming or interesting for you. To add the mindfulness dimension, bring the music into the forefront of your mind rather than allowing it to float around in the background. Pay close attention to each sound or note, focus on the type of sound, the instrument, its depth, its tone, its volume, its pitch, and so on. Listen carefully for variations and changes in the pace and the sound. Experience fully the feelings, the emotions, the sensations which the music is producing in you.

MINDFULNESS AND PANIC ATTACKS

In Chapter 8, panic attacks were explained, and some useful techniques designed to help you cope with them were introduced. The PAUSE routine is one of the key tools for this, and I developed it over 15 years ago from a strategy used almost 40 years ago by an Edinburgh self-help group run by Sheila Crichton. And yet this routine is very much in line with the much younger mindfulness techniques you are learning in this chapter. The acronym PAUSE was used:

▶ *Pause*

▶ *Absorb*

▶ *Use*

▶ *Slowly*

▶ *Ease yourself back.*

Pause is very much saying, come into the here and now. And *Absorb* is all about absorbing detail all around you. Both of these are basic mindfulness processes. So if you feel the beginnings of a panic attack, coming into the here and now, carrying out a mindfulness session until you feel well enough to carry on with whatever you were doing, should also be very effective.

MINDFULNESS AND THERAPY

Although mindfulness as a skill had been around for a long time, the idea of using mindfulness in a therapeutic sense was first studied by Dr John Kabat-Zinn, emeritus Professor of

Medicine at the University of Massachusetts, who began his work on the subject very recently in therapeutic terms, just over 30 years ago. 'Mindfulness-based approaches' are an integration of the ancient Buddhist practices and philosophy of mindfulness, with current psychological understanding and knowledge, which are taught in an entirely secular way, and have no religious context at all.

Things have moved on apace since then, with the National Institute for Clinical Excellence (NICE) now recommending mindfulness-based stress reduction (MBSR), developed by Dr Kabat-Zinn in 1979, and combining mindfulness, meditation, yoga and group discussion. Mindfulness also forms the basis of mindfulness-based cognitive therapy (MBCT).

In the UK, The Centre for Mindfulness Research and Practice (CMRP) is a self-funding organization based in the School of Psychology at Bangor University. CMRP was the first UK organization to establish professional training in the field on mindfulness.*

Focus points

1. Being mindful means spending more time in the *here and now*, and paying attention to one thing at a time, be that your body, your mind, or something or someone around you.
2. Check back over your Personal Journal, and look at how your stress level scores out of ten have varied since you began this book. Update this if needed.
3. Look back at your three lists of changes or things to do *now*, *soon* or *later* on. Update this if needed.
4. In your average day, it would be good to be using a quick relaxation technique (one or two minutes) around four or five times a day, and a longer session of relaxation every day, or every other day. And you could now add to this a short mindfulness session.
5. In your average week, aim to be gradually building-in helpful lifestyle changes, useful changes in thinking habits, and generally mindful behaviours.

10

How NLP can help you beat stress

This chapter will explain more about what neurolinguistic programming (NLP) is, and what it can be used for. And since we are interested principally in stress management, we will explore some of the ideas and techniques from NLP, which are particularly useful when dealing with stress.

Neurolinguistic programming is a relative newcomer to personal development. This intriguing and broad body of knowledge, perspectives and practical techniques, first saw the light of day in the 1970s at the University of California, when a linguist and a mathematician sparked off each other's ideas and produced something greater than the sum of the two parts – an entirely new practical subject concentrating on how the language we use in our thoughts is linked to how we behave. This new school of thought was called 'neurolinguistic programming' or, for short, NLP.

How do you feel?

Here are five key ideas from this chapter to think about now. They will be discussed later:

1 Your new business venture lets you down unexpectedly, or you just can't get to grips with a new hobby, or your last appraisal at work was very disappointing. Which of these is nearest to how you feel?

   a Should have done better

   b Nothing in particular

   c A failure

   d Don't know

   e That what you've learned you'll take forward

2 Which these groups of words would you use most frequently? (Your first reaction is best.)

   a Illustrate, reveal, focus

   b Foundation, tackle, smooth

   c Harmony, remark, discuss

3 How often do you notice a) your own body language, or b) other people's? What does this body language tell you?

4 Do you know what your three main life goals are right now? If so, how did you decide on these?

5 If you had to choose four rules for success in life, what would they be?

NLP and four rules for success

An important part of NLP is the *Four Rules for Success*. These rules can be applied to anything you're doing, and they relate just as much to stress. These Four Rules are:

▶ be aware

▶ be flexible

▶ know what you want, and

▶ take action to get it.

The first of these NLP rules is that we should aim to *be aware*. What this is encouraging us to do is take time to lift our heads from the daily grind, and the stresses and strains of life, and from our narrow and sometimes blinkered focus, to absorb what's all around us. Use all five senses to raise our level of awareness. See possibilities, see the world, listen, really listen to people around us, feel as if we can reach out and touch the tiny specks of dust glinting beautifully in the morning sunshine as it pours through a chink in the curtains. This is similar to mindfulness, which was covered in Chapter 9.

Rule 2 suggests we should also *be flexible*. Be open to new thoughts, new suggestions, other ways of doing what we're doing. If what you're doing doesn't seem to be working, then why not try something else? Don't beat yourself up that this way hasn't worked out. That's just how life works. It's not just you. Try another way, and another if you need to. If you're deep in a rut, you can't see the stars, far less reach for them.

Know what you want is rule 3. That can be so very easy to say, but often so difficult to do. Life can be so busy, that there is never the right time. And what about other people's needs, which we so often place before our own? The bottom line here is that if you don't actually know what you want, there's virtually no chance of you getting it. You won't win the race if you're not even in it. So allow space in your world to put yourself first for a while, and mull over what you want, so that you can choose the steps you need to take to achieve that.

If you want to be less stressed, Rule 4 says *take action* to achieve this. That's what this chapter is all about. NLP can show you how to make changes in your usual behaviour and mindset. The four rules for success is just one part of that.

Since the 1970s, NLP has steadily grown into a very broad body of information and techniques. It has been described and defined in many ways, as it is a particularly varied subject. A linking theme would be that NLP is about the human mind and thinking, and how these function and connect with each other. NLP explores our habitual patterns of thought, and how these translate into our behaviour. It also sets out to show how to change these processes for the better.

Originally conceived as a way of making personal therapy and coaching more effective, NLP is now used by many thousands of people, in areas such as business, sport, personal coaching and education. In practical terms, NLP offers a wide range of straightforward methods, tools, and models, to apply to everything we do, wherever we do it. So we can learn how to improve and enhance our performance, including how we manage stress.

Mythbuster: NLP is very complicated and hard to understand, and it's all about analysing the words we use.

This idea has come about because of its long and complex name, and because many people have heard a little about what NLP says about the kind of words we use a lot. But you'll find in this chapter that you shouldn't judge a book by its cover. NLP is far simpler than its name, and there is much more to it than the words we choose to use regularly.

The close interplay between our thought and behaviour patterns develops as we are growing up, and without us being aware of it, can be affecting everything we do, or try to do as adults. If we observe other people, and we know what to look for, we can notice this interplay in action in them too. So at its most basic, NLP is concerned with how the workings of our mind and the language we use in our thoughts can affect our body and behaviour. It tells us how we can change these for the better, to improve everything we do.

In summary, NLP makes it easier to:

▶ understand ourselves

▶ set realistic goals for ourselves

▶ understand other people better

▶ communicate more effectively with others

▶ improve performance in all aspects of life

▶ achieve our aims in life

▶ reach decisions and make effective changes.

Every item in this list can make stress less likely. Equally, each item will make stress easier to cope with if it does occur.

Remember this

NLP itself is far simpler than any attempt to describe it. Try describing something simple, like a pizza cutter, in a few words, or explaining what you can do with it, without actually having one to hand, and you'll see this for yourself. NLP is just like that. So it's time to take the pizza cutter out of the drawer and show it to you properly. It's time to have a closer look at NLP, and to find out what it can do.

SOME OF NLP'S BASIC ASSUMPTIONS

Although NLP encapsulates many different ideas, and practical uses, it is built on a number of founding beliefs and assumptions, which underlie it and remain constant. These provide a linking thread running through all of NLP. They may seem obvious and banal at first sight, but they actually have profound and far-reaching implications for how we lead our lives.

NLP and our senses

NLP also makes us much more aware of how our senses affect the way we think. But how exactly do we think? When you're choosing the shopping in the supermarket, or discussing next year's budget during a meeting at work, or having a drink with friends, what exactly is going on in your head? We all have a kind of running conversation, or a running commentary going on in our head most of the time. And we do this mainly with words. 'Must get that report finished', or 'Not long until lunchtime', or 'What does he think he's doing!'

If our thoughts include pictures or images too, we are likely to use more visual words when we begin describing to others what we are thinking, or what we have 'in mind'. So our thoughts and speech will contain words and phrases like *I see, my view, in hindsight, illustrate,* or *perspective.* If our thoughts contain sounds or other people's voices, 'auditory' words and phrases may be prominent when we come to pass on a decision or a suggestion to our partner, our boss, or a member of the family. Words and phrases like *out of earshot,* or *in a manner of speaking.* In just the same way, this can apply to the other three senses: touch, smell, and taste.

Remember this

Most people have a preferred way of thinking, and speaking which favours pictures, sounds or bodily sensations such as touch. Fewer people think preferentially in smells or tastes. This preferred way of thinking is called our favoured 'representational system'.

Here are some more examples to help make this new idea clearer.

Jeremy, a postman, has a preference for using words and phrases related to touch, such as 'good to touch base with you', or 'I can't quite put my finger on it'. These are referred to as 'kinaesthetic' words and phrases.

Sinead is a physiotherapist, and is more 'olfactory'. In other words, she tends to use phrases relating to smell, such as 'sweet smell of success', or 'keep your nose out of my business'.

Devindra tends to think in a more visual or auditory way, and uses phrases like 'the way I look at it...' or 'I don't like your tone'.

Keep me in the loop!...

I'll sound him out on that...

I hear what you're saying...

So, there are five main 'representational systems': Visual, Auditory, Kinaesthetic, Olfactory, Gustatory, or VAKOG, for short. Here are some more examples of words and phrases which reflect these. Tick or make a note of any which you use regularly.

System	Examples of words	Examples of phrases
Visual (sight)	Illustrate, insight, focus.	Looking forward to it. Tunnel vision. Keep me in the picture.
Auditory (hearing)	Outspoken, tongue-tied, vocal.	Calling the tune. Sound you out. Turning a deaf ear.
Kinaesthetic (bodily experience/touch/feel)	Grasp, smooth, tactile, rough.	Get to grips with. Hold on a moment. Heavy going.
Olfactory (smell)	Fragrant, aroma, odour.	A nose for it. Coming up roses. Smell a rat.
Gustatory (taste)	Tasty, flavour, sweet, sickly.	Food for thought. A bitter pill to swallow. I've had my fill of this.

Language is inextricably linked with how we think, and is therefore bound to affect how we behave too. This can have all sorts of repercussions. Here are just a few examples:

If one person in a relationship tends to think primarily in a visual way, while the other thinks mainly in a kinaesthetic way, problems and tensions may be created during their conversations. These will be difficult for them to become aware of, and resolve. This is a *perfect recipe* (notice 'perfect recipe' is a gustatory phrase) for stress. Making joint decisions will be particularly difficult.

At work, if half of your team *leans* (kinaesthetic) towards using phrases like, 'keep in touch' or 'when the going gets tough….' (kinaesthetic), whilst the other half are *on a different wavelength* (auditory) and favour expressing themselves through phrases like *sounding board* or *I hear what you're saying* (auditory), this can lead to conflict. Being aware of these subtle differences can enhance relationships and encourage *smooth running* (kinaesthetic) at home and at work.

Likewise, if you can be more *tuned in* to your line manager's use of language, or that of the buyer you are trying to sell your product list to, or even that of your son's teacher, then you'll find it much easier to build a rapport with them, and ultimately, to achieve what you wanted, and so be less stressed in the process.

Remember this

Listening carefully to people talking on radio or television discussion programmes is a good way to practise 'tuning in' to their use of language and whether they prefer to use visual, auditory or kinaesthetic words.

Notice the phrase *tuning in*, from the previous paragraph, is an auditory phrase, and of course the very words *stress*, *tension* or *pressure* are themselves strongly kinaesthetic – as is the word *strongly*, just used in this sentence!

Throughout the book, random use has been made of all the representational systems. So keep your *eyes peeled* (visual), and your *ears pinned back* (auditory), as you are reading, so that you can *get to grips* with this concept (kinaesthetic), and develop *a nose for it* (olfactory). This will definitely give you *food for thought* (gustatory), provide you with an opportunity to practice, and help to give you *a clearer picture* (visual)!

The language of NLP

Even from the little you've learned so far, it's clear that not only does NLP have a lot to say about how people use language, but NLP clearly has a language, or jargon, all of its own. A number of ideas and concepts with fairly complex names have already been introduced. But, rest assured, you don't have to remember any of these names and terms, in order to understand them, or indeed to apply them when dealing with stress. These terms are in this book for those readers with a special interest in NLP and its concepts, or anyone who just likes to hear the whole story.

But this chapter will be no less useful to you, whether or not you remember any of these new terms. The main thing is that you understand what they mean, and how to use the various techniques and ideas to your advantage. This will make your life better and more fulfilling, and as part of that, help you to be more resilient and manage stress better.

KNOWING WHERE YOU'RE GOING – GOALS OR OUTCOMES?

Having clear goals, and knowing how and when you expect to reach them, can help lower the stress in your life. NLP uses the term 'outcome' in preference to 'goal' or 'objective'. This is very significant. A goal is what we aim for, and is something we definitely want, but an outcome is what we actually get as a result of our actions. And this outcome may not be what we were aiming for; it may not be what we wanted. So NLP calls this an 'undesirable outcome'. For those things we really want from life, NLP uses the term 'desirable outcome'.

NLP also suggests that a desirable outcome should be a 'well-formed outcome'. What this means is that the outcome should:

► Be stated in the positive – 'I want...', rather than 'I don't want...'

► Be within your control.

► Be clear and specific.

► Be within your ability (skills, and resources).

► Not produce negative outcomes as a by-product.

► A clear first step.

Try it now

To help generate goals, try 'brainstorming'. You may be familiar with this already. All you do is relax your mind and allow it to freely come up with goals – and just note them down as they come, without judging, criticizing or commenting. Start with the obvious goals, then let your mind wander totally unrestricted, and allow it to think 'outside the box'.

Knowing where you're going – life audit

Taking your eye off the small stuff, and seeing the big picture is a crucial part of knowing where you're headed, and feeling you have some control over your life. A 'life audit' is one way of doing that. It's just like an audit of your finances, but it explores your life in all its aspects. You'll need about thirty minutes to an hour to do this.

1 Place one of these ten headings at the top of a separate blank page in your Personal Journal:

   ▶ Your family

   ▶ Personal relationships

   ▶ Where you live

   ▶ Friends and social life

   ▶ Work or career

   ▶ Money

   ▶ Your health

   ▶ Fun and recreation

   ▶ Personal growth and learning

   ▶ Inner soul and spirit.

2 Now think about each heading, and without analysing it for too long, score it out of ten, for how happy you are with it (ten being full marks) – and write your score next to the heading.

3 Next, under each heading, write a list of anything about that heading you're not happy with and would like to change. Give this a bit of thought, but don't agonize over it. Three or four at the most. No more than half a page.

4 Next, write a new heading, 'GOALS', in the centre of the page.

5 Thinking about these things you're unhappy with, write down under this heading any ideas or GOALS you have for making the changes needed to improve matters, and roughly when you would prefer to complete this – your 'goals' or outcomes, in other words.

6 Look over all ten pages, and thinking about what you've written, choose two areas of your life you would elect to improve first. This might be those with the lowest scores out of ten – but it might not be.

7 Now for those two aspects of your life, look over the goals you've written down, and underline the first two or three you would like to start working towards achieving. Have another think about the time-frame you've given – is this sensible, and is it feasible? If not, change that now.

YOUR 'HAPPINESS QUOTIENT' (HQ)

Taken as a whole, the ten scores in your Life Audit provide an overview of your life, and a picture of which parts of it you are most and least happy with. This gives a Happiness Profile (HP). And, if you add up all ten scores, this will give you an idea of your 'Happiness Quotient', scored out of 100. Here is an example:

Name: James, Analytical Scientist, age 46	
Area of life	HAPPINESS PROFILE (How happy with it from 0 to 10)
Your family	6
Personal relationships	6
Where you live	7
Friends and social life	3
Work or career	4
Money	7
Your health	7
Fun and recreation	5
Personal growth and learning	5
Inner soul and spirit	5
Two aspects to improve first	Friends and social life Work or career
HAPPINESS QUOTIENT	55

This audit process is something you can come back to on a regular basis, say once every month or two, to check on your progress, and continue fine-tuning and improving each area of your life.

What really matters to you?

Even when you've sorted out your goals and desired outcomes, it can still be hard to know where to start. And you can waste so much time just trying to choose a starting point. One way of looking at it is to start anywhere, as long as you just start. This is far and away better than continuing to do nothing in a kind of limbo state. A better way is to sort out your priorities. Here is one way you can do this. Write these four headings across the top of a clean sheet of paper:

▶ Not urgent and not important

▶ Urgent but not important

▶ Not urgent but important

▶ Both urgent and important.

Give each of your goals from your Life Audit a number, beginning with 1. For each item on your list of goals, think about it carefully, and write the number under one of these four headings.

This means that the goals under the heading 'Both Urgent and Important' are your priorities, followed by 'Important Not Urgent'.

Watch out for a long list in the 'Both Urgent and Important' column. This is going to mean you're under too much pressure, and this may be causing you stress – can any of these items move to another heading? Are they truly urgent and important? Maybe their targets are too optimistic, and you need to be more realistic in how much time you give yourself to do things?

CAN YOU WALK THE WALK?

From a more practical point of view, paying attention to how we appear to others can be worth doing. Do you look stressed or nervous? You may look unapproachable because you seem unsure or under pressure. Or do you look as if you lack confidence? Any of these impressions will make stressful encounters with others more likely. Assertiveness touched on this in an earlier chapter, but there's more NLP can add to this:

▶ Find a current photograph or video of yourself. Or just look at yourself in a full length mirror. Look closely and honestly.

▶ Imagine you've never seen this person before. Take a step back mentally.

▶ What are your first overall impressions?

▶ What sort of message is your appearance giving to others?

▶ What about your posture? How are you standing?

▶ Your voice? The way you dress? How will others react? Be honest.

▶ Which of these messages are you reasonably happy with?

▶ What improvements or changes would you like to make?

▶ What would you do first?

Try it now

Here are some more ideas on how to make your body appear more confident and assured, as this will improve your dealings with others, and help lower your stress. Even if you already feel you look confident, there will be something here for you:

✳ Take a few moments when on your own, to practise standing or sitting in a relaxed way. Use a relaxation or breathing technique from earlier in the book to help you.

✳ A relaxed, open posture is best most of the time. Open posture means comfortably upright, shoulders comfortably down, head up.

✳ Try not to fold your arms as this creates a barrier, and can be interpreted as a lack of interest, or disagreement

✳ Nerves and lack of confidence can make you form a fist with your hands, or cling to a handbag, briefcase or drink, like a comfort blanket. People do notice this. It's time to let go.

✳ When sitting, sit up well. Slouching looks defensive, and lacks a professional look, so sit up and lean forward a little towards others. This shows interest.

MATCHING AND MIRRORING

This technique is probably one of the best known, and oldest of NLP techniques:

Next time you're amongst other people in a shop or on a train, look carefully at their body language, without making this obvious.

Without hearing a word of their conversation, can you can see which people have a rapport going?

Pairs or groups of people who feel a connection with each other will unconsciously mirror the other's body language, and speech style, without being aware they're doing it.

So, if you want to create rapport quickly, you can do this by matching and mirroring the body language of the other person.

Remember this

To make sure matching and mirroring isn't glaringly obvious, and seems natural, wait 20–30 seconds after you've seen a person's change of posture before matching it, and don't make your body language identical, just make it similar. Try just matching the upper or lower body, rather than all of it. Like everything else in this book, make sure to use this technique with integrity and respect. There's a fine line between mirroring and mimicry. So take great care with this.

THERE IS NO FAILURE, ONLY FEEDBACK

This thought is one of the most well known in NLP. It's all about changing how you think about so-called 'failures' in life. No one decides on their goals just once in life. It's a moving and adapting process which never stops. Priorities change. Needs change. And sometimes we can make ill informed choices, or our values and priorities can simply change. So our goals need to be able to be changed too, without feeling we've made a mistake. Because we haven't. There are no mistakes, and no failure, only feedback. And this feedback will help us to constantly fine tune and adapt our goals and targets.

A FEW WORDS TO FINISH

Whatever you do, don't rush out to take a crack at all this before you're ready. Remember you need to practise most of the NLP skills we've talked about, before letting them loose suddenly on your friends, family and colleagues. As with everything else in this book, take these new skills on board one at a time, build them into your Personal Journal, and try them out first in situations which aren't too important, and then you'll be ready for the off, when the time is right.

Focus points

1. Be sure of what you want:

   * Think about and plan this carefully.
   * Priorities can be worked out depending on how urgent and how important your goal is.
   * NLP practitioners often use the term 'outcome' in preference to 'goal', as it is describing what you actually achieved, rather than what was being aimed at.
   * Plan your 'outcomes' in a clear, realistic and positive way, and think through their effects on all areas of your life.
   * As soon as you are fixed on an 'outcome', in other words, you know what you want, you should decide on your first step, and act on it.
   * Using the four rules formula for success (awareness, flexibility, know what you want, take action to get it), gives you the greatest chance of achieving your desired outcomes.
   * Focus on the solutions, not on the problems.
   * If what you're doing isn't working, do something else.

2. Open up your senses and observe everything:

   * Notice all input from all of your senses, and observe detail.
   * Study other people's everyday patterns of thought, language, learning and behaviour, and harmonize yours with these.
   * Check out others people's dominant representational system (word usage) and match these.
   * Observe and decide what 'mood' or 'state' others are in, and react accordingly.

3. Think about body language:

   * Always think about your own body language and the body language you see in others.
   * Use your appearance, body language and voice to give the impression you want to give.
   * Use simple relaxation and breathing techniques to calm you.
   * Match and mirror body language, voice and general demeanour to enhance rapport – but do this with care and integrity.
   * Speak at the same pace, and look out for favourite phrases and words of the other person, and subtly use these yourself.

4. Create rapport with others

   * There are 4Cs to getting your message across: calm, confident and constructive communication.
   * 'Small-talk' is the usual starting point for rapport – be prepared for this.
   * Be genuinely interested in people. Be friendly, smile and listen.
   * Aim for a conversation with rhythm, enthusiasm and momentum of its own.
   * Like and respect others, and be genuine, consistent and positive.
   * Avoid dominating the conversation, not listening properly, or interrupting.

5. How did it go?

   * Afterwards, review how things went: did you get what you wanted? Did you reach a 'win-win' agreement? What went well? What wasn't so good?
   * Remember the NLP mantra: 'No mistakes, only feedback'.
   * Remember the NLP fundamental idea that 'underlying every behaviour, there is a positive intention'.
   * Decide what you want to take forward to the next time, if there's anything you need to practice more, and what you would do differently next time.
   * Onwards and upwards!

11

Alternative and complementary therapies

This chapter will introduce some of the most common and most effective alternative and complementary therapies from ancient to modern, which also have research or strong anecdotal evidence suggesting that they directly encourage relaxation. Wherever possible, self-help techniques are also included as a taster. It's really all about finding which can work for you, falls within your budget, and can fit easily into your life.

Mind and body in harmony*

Being able to relax for short or long periods is probably the most important factor in managing stress better, and building resilience and cushioning for the long term. So far, ways of relaxing the body and mind have been described, and these have been very much from a medical, physiological or psychological background. But there are many techniques for relaxing which come under the umbrella of alternative and complementary therapies (ACT). These are often much more holistic in their approach, aiming to relax the whole body, mind and self.

Space doesn't allow for including all ACTs that can aid relaxation, as there are so many. Almost all ACTs can have a relaxing aspect to them, even if it's just because quality time is being spent doing something enjoyable or peaceful in supportive and interesting company. There is more information about other ACTs, in the Optional extras.

If you do decide to try out any of these therapies, it's very important to make sure the therapist or practitioner is fully qualified in their particular field. Going on personal recommendation, or contacting only practitioners who are members of an established and recognized professional group, are good strategies.

How do you feel?

Here are five key ideas from this chapter to think about now. They will be discussed later:

1 Have you ever used an alternative or complementary therapy?

   a Yes

   b No

   c Don't know

2 If you haven't, why not? If you have, what were you looking for, and did you find it helpful for this?

3 If you were going to use an ACT, would you prefer:

   a A therapist

   b Self-help

   c To become a therapist or practitioner yourself

   d Don't know

   e Other

4 Do you know how to check out a therapist or practitioner's background and qualifications?

   a Yes

   b No

   c Not sure

5 Do you have a pet? If so, does the pet make any difference to your stress? If you don't have a pet, do you think having one would make you more or less stressed?

T'ai chi

T'ai chi (pronounced 'ty chee') was created on the basis of nature and harmony, and consists of a sequence of graceful flowing movements and deep breathing exercises designed to encourage relaxation, inner calm and mental balance. It has been called 'meditation in motion'. T'ai chi aims to achieve harmony with nature and the balance of mental serenity and physical strength. Most people find that attending a class with a teacher makes it more enjoyable and easier to learn.

It has been in use for hundreds of years, having originated in China as a martial art. In the non-competitive type, movements are performed slowly with relaxed muscles and the mind focussed on each step. There are more than 100 possible movements and positions to choose from. These are not intended to be strenuous or muscle-building, but to gently exercise the body, calm the mind and stimulate the internal organs. T'ai chi is well known for its various specific movements and poses. It is thought that the slow, rhythmic movements of the body help calm the mind, relax the muscles and nervous system, and if practised daily, this can have a lasting effect.

Remember this

T'ai chi is a non-physical form of exercise, so is suitable for any age. As well as producing relaxation, the postures and movements improve muscle tone, flexibility and balance.

Therapy from pets

Research shows that stroking a friendly cat or dog, especially if it's your own companion, has a relaxing effect and can even lower blood pressure. Petting an animal for just a couple of minutes helps relieve stress.

It's not just cats and dogs which can have this relaxing effect. Any pet companion will have the same positive effect: rabbit, budgie, hamster, and so on. Even watching fish swimming around a fish tank has been shown to have beneficial effects, including relaxation and lowered blood pressure. Although for most people the idea of companionship and relaxation provided

by pets conjures up an image of a furry domestic animal, an interesting study by Eddy ('RM and Beaux: Reductions in cardiac activity in response to a pet snake.' *Journal of Nervous and Mental Disease*, 1996, **184** (9), 573–5.) provides evidence that attachment to any species is likely to elicit favourable physiological responses in pet owners. Eddy studied relaxation responses and reported that for a snake owner, stroking a pet snake produced greater reductions in blood pressure than stroking a cat or a dog.

Deciding to keep a pet, is not a decision to take without thinking, so think carefully before getting a pet mainly for relaxation purposes. They can vary a great deal in their disposition, and owning a pet brings not just relaxation, but many expenses, and extra work to be done. However, owning a dog will mean regular walks in the fresh air, and chatting to others owners. All of these also have a relaxing effect.

Yoga

The word yoga means 'union' in Sanskrit, which is the language of ancient India where yoga originated. The name relates to the union between the mind, body and spirit yoga can bring. What is commonly referred to as 'yoga' in the West can be more accurately described by the Sanskrit word 'asana', which refers to the part of yoga involving the practice of physical postures or poses. Yoga promotes total relaxation of body and mind through concentrating on these specific movements and poses, such as the Lion or the Cat.

You can do yoga for yourself at home using a DVD or a book, or you can go to a class locally, which may also include breathing exercises, or basic meditation, and often finishes with a peaceful session of Total Relaxation.

Mythbuster

It is commonly thought that you have to be involved in some sort of religion to do yoga. This is not the case.

YOGA BREATHING

Called 'Pranayama' in Sanskrit, yoga breathing can be done alongside yoga poses or just while sitting quietly. Alternate Nostril Breathing is one of the most well-known yoga breathing exercises, and is relaxing, and calming, but maintains alertness at the same time.

Try it now

Alternate nostril breathing

1 Make yourself comfortable, in an upright position.
2 With your right hand, bring your thumb to the right side of your nose and your index finger to the left side.
3 Now gently close off your right nostril with your thumb.
4 Inhale through your left nostril, in your own time.
5 Now close off your left nostril with your index finger, allowing your right nostril to open again.
6 Exhale through your right nostril in your own time.
7 Inhale through your right nostril.
8 Close off your right nostril with your thumb, allowing your left nostril to open.
9 Exhale through your left nostril.
10 Inhale through your left nostril.
11 Repeat the cycle five to ten times.

Massage*

Massage therapy originated about 2,000 years ago, in China, and is predominantly associated with its health benefits. But it is also very relaxing. Massage can be performed by several types of health care professionals, such as a physiotherapist, occupational therapist or massage therapist, but even a back or neck rub from a friend or your partner has the same effect.

Many versions of massage exist, from shiatsu, to aromatherapy, Swedish, hot stone, Indian head massage, chair massage, to name just a few. There isn't space to cover every type of massage here, but a broad overview of what this technique has to offer is given. If you want to find out more, see Optional extras.

MASSAGE ON THE GO

Shoulder and neck massages are now on offer in most airport departure lounges, and also in many shopping malls. Many employers provide this kind of massage in the workplace as an aid to relieving tension and stress, sometimes at break times, and sometimes during working hours. Chair massage may be given in a private room or corner of the office, with the employee fully clothed, seated upright using a special chair, sometimes with the head leaning forward resting on a special support. The massage would be done on the shoulders, neck and upper back, and would last 10–15 minutes. Alternatively, this is sometimes now provided during working hours and fully clothed at the employee's desk, one afternoon a week, or on-call.

Reflexology*

Reflexology involves applying pressure to the feet and hands with specific thumb, finger and hand techniques without the use of oil or lotion. Though reflexology has a whole range of specific medical purposes, for the purposes of this book, the main effect which concerns us here is that if you enjoy someone working with your feet, this encourages bodily relaxation, and soothes tired feet.

Reflexology can be traced back as far as China and India in the third millennium BC, and Japan around 700 BC. It has become a very popular alternative therapy over the past few decades. Reflexology can easily be done without a therapist's help, using a range of balls, textured surfaces, and special rollers that are easy to find in the shops. You can either roll your feet over them on the floor, or stand on them in the shower. Alternatively, you can ask a friend or partner for a foot massage, or even do it yourself.

Acupuncture*

Acupuncture has been likened to the effect of tranquilizers, with a quick and lasting effect, and it has been suggested that it can also cause a decrease in fast delta brain waves and an increase in the slower alpha brain waves that are associated with relaxation. Research has shown how acupuncture can lessen both the frequency and severity of muscle tension headaches and migraines, and there is evidence of a calming effect too.

Acupuncture is the ancient art of inserting very fine needles into special places called acupuncture points in the body. It is thought to have originated in China five thousand years ago, but there are also traces of it in Japan, Tibet and Korea. These needles are carefully and essentially painlessly inserted into the acupuncture points to relieve a range of pains, diseases and conditions. But, acupuncture can also be calming and relaxing.

You don't have to understand how acupuncture works for it to be relaxing, but it is based on the idea that the body has an energy force running through it known as Qi (roughly pronounced Chee). Qi travels throughout the body along 'Meridians' or special pathways. The acupuncture points are specific locations where the Meridians come to the surface of the skin, and are easily accessible by acupuncture.

ACUPRESSURE
Acupuncture is a skilled and delicate process, and is not really something you can do for yourself. However, there is an alternative to acupuncture which doesn't use needles. This is

called acupressure, and it works by stimulating the same points as acupuncture, but with fingers, or sometimes special bands instead of needles. You can buy wristbands for travel sickness, or morning sickness which put pressure on acupuncture points in the wrists. But you can also use acupressure on yourself.

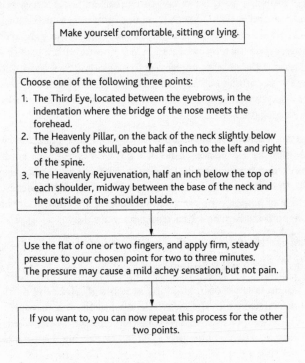

Make yourself comfortable, sitting or lying.

Choose one of the following three points:

1. The Third Eye, located between the eyebrows, in the indentation where the bridge of the nose meets the forehead.
2. The Heavenly Pillar, on the back of the neck slightly below the base of the skull, about half an inch to the left and right of the spine.
3. The Heavenly Rejuvenation, half an inch below the top of each shoulder, midway between the base of the neck and the outside of the shoulder blade.

Use the flat of one or two fingers, and apply firm, steady pressure to your chosen point for two to three minutes. The pressure may cause a mild achey sensation, but not pain.

If you want to, you can now repeat this process for the other two points.

Alexander Technique

The Alexander Technique applies to your daily activities, such as sitting, standing, walking, lifting and speaking. It can help you do all these without unnecessary tension. This is similar to the 'Partial Relaxation' included in Chapter 5. There is lots of overlap and crossover between different methods of relaxing, whether ancient or modern, simple or high tech. And that's a good sign that you're doing something effective, as it's showing up in lots of very different places.

This particular technique was developed by Frederick Matthias Alexander (1869–1955), who was an actor. He developed chronic laryngitis while performing, and wanted to solve this problem. He carefully watched himself while speaking, and noticed that the muscles in his neck were tense when he spoke, and that this was probably the cause of his vocal problem. So, he developed the Alexander Technique (AT) named after him, which is another method of releasing unwanted muscular tension throughout the body, especially tension caused by poor posture from a lifetime of tensing the muscles in reaction to many of life's worries and concerns, causing posture to deteriorate and produce unnecessary tension. This technique is also useful for improving awareness of balance and co-ordination.

An AT teacher will show you how to release this 'unnecessary and habitual muscle tension', especially if it has built up very gradually over a number of years and you're not even aware that it's there at all. All of this is best done working with a trained AT teacher, who is able to pinpoint the exact postural changes needed, and who can give practical help and advice on how to do this.

You can try it for yourself too:

You'll need a full length mirror for this.

1 Stand in front of it, and look at yourself. Notice in particular the relationship of your whole head to the rest of your body. Notice how this relationship changes as you perform simple activities like talking, standing, sitting, lifting a book, holding a cup, walking a few steps around the room.

2 Now, try changing how your head and body are positioned relative to each other, perhaps tilting it a little forward or backward from the top of your neck and see if these small changes make any difference to how you are breathing, moving or standing.

3 Alexander found that the most useful change he could make was to mentally direct his neck to be free of tension so that his head would balance lightly at the top of the spine.

4 Try this for yourself. Does anything look different? Does anything feel different?

5 Next, try doing the opposite of what Alexander suggests. Stiffen your neck a little. What effect does this have on how easy it is to breathe, or the position of your head, or carrying out simple activities like lifting up a book, or saying a few words?

Reiki

Reiki can be used for relaxation, and managing stress, and is also associated with general healing. The name Reiki has come from the Japanese pronunciation of two Chinese letters, or 'characters' that are said to describe the energy itself: 'rei' (meaning 'spirit', 'soul' or 'ghost') and 'ki' ('energy' or 'life force'). Reiki uses touch, and is based on the idea that an unseen 'life force energy' flows through us and gives us life. Reiki energy is channelled through the practitioner, directly into the client. If your 'life force energy' is low, you're more likely to get sick or feel stress, and if it is high, it's more likely you will be happy, relaxed and healthy.

Key idea

Training as a Reiki practitioner is not taught in the usual sense. Knowledge is transferred to the student during a Reiki class, which is given by a Reiki master.

During the training, the Reiki student also has the opportunity to tap into an unlimited supply of 'life force energy' to improve health and enhance the quality of life. While Reiki is spiritual in nature, it is not a religion. As in other therapies, there is nothing you must believe in order to benefit from it, so it is available to everyone.

Reiki practitioners work in various places, such as complementary health centres, or health and fitness centres, or many work from home. They often rely completely on word of mouth from their regular clients to contact others. If you decide to contact a therapist, you will find that very few advertise their services in the conventional way, such as in telephone directories or on-line. Another way to do it is to take a first level course, which lasts two or three days, and as part of it, you acquire life force energy from the Reiki master, and learn how to use Reiki on yourself.

Are you having a laugh?

It is now realized that humour, laughter, and even just smiling can help people manage stress better, and feel more relaxed and resilient. A recent study showed that pre-school-aged children laugh up to 400 times a day, but by the time we reach adulthood, we laugh a mere 17 times per day on average! So there is definitely room for improvement.

Laughter actually reduces the physical effects of stress, and gives a physical and emotional release, which helps to relieve all sorts of tension, and promote relaxation. Surprisingly, a belly laugh can even encourage muscle relaxation. It does this in two steps. First, while you're laughing, the muscles which aren't involved in the laugh, relax. Then, after you finish the belly laugh, the muscles involved in the laughter start to relax.

Even a smile will cause the brain to release endorphins, the feel-good hormones, while the level of the stress hormone, cortisol, is reduced. In fact, just using the muscles which make you smile, even in a 'put-on', rather than a genuine smile, starts to release endorphins. According to the International Stress Management Association UK, smiling is the first line of defence against tension and stress.

Case study

I have a friend, Pamela, and I've known her for years (I've changed her name here). Every time I see her, whoever she's with seems to be smiling or laughing, because she is. And she doesn't have an easy life. She's just always on the lookout for amusing, happy or funny things happening, and seldom misses one to tell everyone about, and this reminds them of their own amusing stories, and so it goes on. Everyone she meets goes away with a healthy shot of happy brain chemicals to share with other people.

HOW TO BRING MORE HUMOUR INTO YOUR LIFE

An opinion poll for *The Happiness Formula* series on BBC Two, in 2006 found that Britain is less happy than in the 1950s – despite the fact that we are three times richer. The proportion of people saying they are 'very happy' had fallen from 52 per cent in 1957 to just 36 per cent. Studies have even shown that humour can give us a more light-hearted perspective and help us view stressful events as 'challenges', rather than threats, so that they seem less of a problem.

We can all bring more happiness, humour and laughter into our lives. This is very much down to personal preferences, as humour is very individual, but here are some suggestions:

▶ Watch really funny or light-hearted television programmes. Choose the comedy film over the weepy or gritty.

▶ Have some comedy DVDs on the shelf, so you can watch one whenever you want. There's everything from comedy classic films, to funny video clips, to sport's most amusing moments, and an endless list of stand-up comedians.

▶ Accept invitations to go out with friends, for a meal or a drink, as lively chat is usually a part of that. But make sure they are cheerful friends.

▶ Limit the amount of time you spend watching news programmes to about 15 minutes a day.

▶ Mark Twain, the American writer (1835–1910), said that the best way to cheer yourself up is to cheer someone else up.

▶ Read a funny book, rather than a thriller or horror.

▶ Let go. Splash about in the pool or bake something messy with the children.

▶ Have a party for your birthday, for a special holiday, or just for fun. All of these encourage a positive and cheerful atmosphere.

▶ Make friends with positive, happy people, and spend time with them.

▶ Learn to see the funny side of situations.

▶ Look for the amusing around you – these aren't usually hard to find if you start to look for them.

▶ Listen closely to those friends who are good at telling funny stories from their everyday life. How do they do it? Where do they find these stories? Work it out and copy it. The effects of this can be dramatic.

And even if you don't feel like it, you can still put on a smile. Research shows that the same beneficial effects happen even if you don't 'feel' the smile. People often call this a smile that doesn't reach the eyes. The positive effects are activated by the muscles used to smile. Smile to yourself, smile at yourself, smile at other people. This will encourage more, and more, completely natural smiles to come, and with them, more contentment and relaxation.

Focus points

1. There are many ACTs which can help you to relax and build resilience.
2. Many of these ACTs can be used as self-help.
3. Always check the background of a therapist or practitioner, and the ACT on offer, before going ahead. Personal recommendations help too.
4. Having a pet can reduce stress.
5. Everyday behaviour such as humour, laughter and smiling can relieve stress too.

12

How to cope with stress anywhere, anytime

An armoury of techniques and approaches for managing stress have been covered so far, and these will help you through any stressful situation you find yourself in. This chapter will give you some additional practical guidance for some of the most common stressful situations, such as the workplace, giving a presentation, exams, or going for an interview. That way you have the best of both worlds. You will be better positioned to deal with the stress, and you'll also have some specialist know-how about the situation itself.

How **do you feel?**

Here are five key ideas from this chapter to think about now. They will be discussed later:

1 Before you read this book, how did you handle stressful situations?

2 If you work in any capacity (paid, unpaid, voluntary, as a carer), or are not working at the moment (job seeker, retired, disabled) does this make you stressed?

   a Never

   b Occasionally

   c Frequently

   d All the time

   e Don't know

   f Other

3 If you answered that you are stressed in Question 2, what do you feel is the reason for this stress? If you answered that you are not stressed, why do you think this is?

4 Which of these situations can be stressful for you? (Choose all that apply.)

   a An interview

   b An appraisal

   c Giving a talk

   d Speaking up at a meeting

   e Making a presentation

   f Making a speech

   g Visiting the dentist

   h Exams or tests

   i Flying

   j Chairing a meeting

k None of the above

l Others

5 Thinking of the situations that are stressful for you, how stressed are you? (Choose all that apply, or give your own answer.):

a It varies

b Slightly stressed mostly

c Moderately stressed mostly

d Very stressed mostly

e Sometimes slightly, sometimes moderately, sometimes very stressed

f Don't know

g Other

Mythbuster

It is a myth that a bit of stress is good for you in stressful situations. What this idea is really saying is that you need to be alert and geared up appropriately for what is being asked of you, not laid-back, half-asleep and apathetic. You want to be geared up for what you have to do, but no more. Any amount of stress is bad news.

Stress at work

Stress caused by work is extremely common. As we saw earlier, time off work due to stress has increased every decade since the 1950s. Most of this is a result of changes in the way life and work are organized today, and unfortunately, this is largely outside your control. Added to this most of the day-to-day causes of work stress are not easy for you to tackle without there being repercussions for your job, business or career. This all adds to the stress, and you can feel trapped and powerless.

No matter what the job is, if it doesn't match your interests and personality, you will feel stressed by it. The outgoing person, who thrives on new activities and meeting new people, would probably find work as a laboratory technician or truck driver hard to cope with. The shrinking violet would probably find life as a double-glazing salesperson or actor impossible.

The dilemma today is that people are often obliged to take whatever job they can find, whether it suits their personality or not. And jobs are no longer static, in the way that they used to be. Jobs change, sometimes rapidly, and often out of all recognition. Employers want a flexible workforce, and with the threat of unemployment, people have little choice but to accept changes to their jobs.

Here is a selection of common causes of work stress – do any of these apply to you? Tick or make a note of all that apply. Is there something else about work which is making you stressed? Think about whether you can actually do something about what is stressing you without unwanted repercussions.

CAUSES OF STRESS

The job

- feel trapped or powerless
- very tight deadlines
- role not clear
- role conflict
- inability to get a job finished
- difficult clients
- unable to do the job effectively
- too many new developments or new technology
- colleagues who aren't competent
- insufficient training
- emotional involvement with clients

- responsibilities of the job
- moving home often
- boring or repetitive.

Working conditions

- unsocial or long hours
- body's natural rhythms upset by shift work
- insecurity and uncertainty
- poor status, low pay,
- no career advancement or promotion prospects
- poor back-up
- unnecessary rules and regulations
- unpredictable hours
- long or disagreeable journey to work
- working from home
- taking work home
- amount of travelling
- ease of being contacted – e-mail, fax, bleepers, car-phones, mobile phones – even at home and out of hours
- overwork or underwork
- not stretched
- time pressure, especially if prolonged
- lack of variety
- demands made on private and social life
- doing job below level of competence
- attending meetings
- irregular hours.

The working environment

► lack of space to work

► noisy, cold or cramped conditions

► excessive heat or humidity

► presence of toxic or dangerous materials

► too many or too few people around you.

Your employer

► ethos difficult for you

► organizational problems

► your beliefs conflicting with your employer's

► staff shortages – you're overloaded

► personality clashes

► no clear strategy

► no clear direction.

Your management

► uncomfortable with management style

► clashing with managers

► inadequate leadership

► manager makes mistakes

► personality clashes

► manager less experienced than you

► being monitored or recorded some or all of the time

► no clear direction

► no mention of your positive contribution

► too much negative criticism.

Your subordinates or team

- constant personnel changes
- inadequate training for you, or them
- clashes or difficulties with them
- having to tell them off
- insufficient time for meetings and discussion
- one difficult person in particular.

Communication with others

- conflict with colleagues
- isolation
- bullying
- poor communication or none
- unnecessary battles.

Problems particularly affecting women

- may be first woman in the job
- woman in a man's world
- promotion difficult
- travelling or staying in hotels alone
- being conspicuously different
- juggling career and home or family
- settling for a 'lesser' job to fit with family responsibilities
- sexism and sexual harassment
- male colleagues can feel threatened.

Your attitudes, expectations and personality

- you have a low tolerance for stress
- you're too passive

- you're too aggressive
- don't enjoy team working
- dislike change
- intolerant of certain behaviours in others, e.g. tidiness, punctuality
- perfectionist
- Type A personality
- lack of confidence
- impatient

Cushioning yourself

There are often no easy answers to these stresses, and there can be consequences for your career or job if you tackle things head on at work.

The most common way people deal with stress at work, is probably to cushion themselves from it by building resilience. These are summarized in the following table:

SKILL	Chapters
Relaxation: body and mind	2, 5, 6, 7, 9,10, 11, 13
Breathing techniques	2,5,6,
Healthy thinking	7,9,10
Good social support	2,4
Taking breaks	4
Healthy lifestyle	4
Leisure	4
Exercise and activity	4
Getting a good night's sleep	6
Assertiveness	7
Coping with panic attacks	8
Mindfulness	9
Neurolinguistic programming (NLP)	10
Work/life balance, build resilience and cushioning	3,4, 9,10,11,13,14

But here are some other thoughts and questions to think about. Tick or make a note of anything you think is relevant to you, decide how to tackle it, and use your Personal Journal to keep on track:

▶ Your thinking habits might be contributing to your stress: this is often very relevant to work stress.

▶ Are you using coping strategies that are making matters worse? E.g. skipping lunch or tea-breaks, taking fewer holidays, taking work home, working harder, faster and longer?

▶ If you're tired, or over-tired, or rushed, or feel stressed, you get less done and do it less well, with more mistakes. Having even a short break every few hours, and longer relaxing breaks on a weekly basis means you have a rest and your nervous system has time to wind down, breaking into the build-up of stress. You'll work more efficiently, and be more productive overall – and you will feel less stressed.

▶ What about learning some new skills? Would that help? Jobs are changing so fast, and a course can help you to keep up. What about assertiveness, confidence building, time management, team working, delegation, management skills. Can you take courses like this at work or outside of it? Can you read up on it?

▶ What about confidential counselling at work? Occupational Health staff are usually trained to help, in confidence. Many employers now provide this entirely separately and independently of the workplace, through an Employee Assistance Programme.

▶ Maybe bullying is a problem. Or discrimination, or sexual harassment? What is your employer's policy and procedures for this? Is an independent helpline or other support available?

Remember this

Your Personal Journal

Keep the Personal Journal you began in Chapter 4 up to date, with your daily stress scores, brief description of each week, and your three lists of changes and new techniques you plan to implement *now*, *soon* or *later*, and continue moving these forward. When the time is right, you can move items in *soon*, into *now*, and those from *later* into *soon*....and so on.

Case study

Read through what's been happening to Lateefa, and make a note of what you think she could do to improve things.

Lateefa is 52 with three grown-up children, two of whom live nearby. She has two grandsons aged three and five whom she loves spending time with. She used to enjoy her work in administration, and got on well with her line manager, Barbara-Ann. She was very settled in her work, and worked on her own initiative a lot of the time. Barbara-Ann then retired and after a reorganization, Lateefa has now joined a team for the first time, with a new team leader, Christopher who is 28. Lateefa now finds that Christopher is always finding fault with her work, and seems to go out of his way to make her feel small in front of colleagues. He seems to want changes all the time and Lateefa can't see why he has to do this. This has gone on for six months, and every day has become difficult, with some incident or other between her and Christopher. Lateefa is separated from her husband and supports herself, so her job is very important to her financially. She now dreads work each day, and wakes in the early hours with a churning stomach and can't get back to sleep. This is making her so tired that she's not getting out much these days. She's also having frequent headaches, and just this week had her first panic attack.

Lateefa's situation is typical of many others. Her job was predictable and enjoyable, and she knew where she was. But then everything changed, and that can be very stressful, especially when you're being criticized, having to work in a team for the first time, and don't feel you have a stake in what's going on, or an understanding of it. Having a younger manager for the first time, can also be difficult. Many processes are going on here. Lateefa is finding the change difficult, especially the loss of a familiar face, and with a young enthusiastic manager the same age as her son, has to come to terms with the fact she's not as young as she was. She's also worried that if things get worse, she may lose her job, which she is financially dependent on. What can she do? From what we've covered in the book, here are some ideas of:

► Take a course in team working.

► Learn to be assertive and how to deal with criticism.

- Each week, the new face and system will be more familiar and less of a threat.

- Her work/life balance is not supporting her in this situation. The comfortable rug has been pulled from under her, and she now needs to cushion herself, and build her resilience and self-confidence. She is on her own at home, so some carefully chosen new leisure pursuits and activities could make her feel younger again, build her confidence, and provide some much needed social support.

Other stressful situations

There are many everyday situations which can be stressful for many people, and we'll look at some of the most common in the remainder of this chapter. For some people, anxiety and tension can begin well before the actual event. Interviews, driving tests or other exams, dealing with an authority figure, and making a presentation or speech are covered in detail, but the same general principles can be applied to any situation which can cause tension, e.g. a dentist appointment, court appearance, or going in to hospital for an operation.

The approach will be a dual one. You'll learn specific skills for each situation. These, along with the stress management skills learned so far, will let you approach the situation in a far more confident and relaxed way. Whatever the situation that is causing stress, preparation is essential.

GETTING READY FOR THOSE STRESSFUL OCCASIONS

We all have those situations which seem to press all the wrong buttons for us. But whatever situation it is that raises our stress level, there are many ways to prepare for it in a way which should ease the anxiety. This shouldn't be left until the day, or the day before though. Just as for any important event, preparations can begin days or even weeks ahead. Reading this book, and this chapter is the first step. What's next?

RELAX

Choose one or two methods of relaxing quickly covered already in the book, which can be done anywhere and isn't noticeable, and which works for you. Practise these, so that you're ready to use either of them on the day. Sometimes the method you had planned just doesn't do it for you on the day. These things can happen. So it's good to have a reserve to pull out of the hat.

As soon as your anxiety about the event kicks in, which may be hours, days or even weeks before the event, use any form of mental and physical relaxation, for at least 10–15 minutes a day, to reduce your tension and anxiety. The more anxious you are, the more often and longer you should relax in this way. You can also do a quick relaxation session for a minute or two, every so often throughout the day. This can really help keep the anxiety levels down.

If your anxiety is still high enough to be distressing, despite regular relaxation, speak to your GP, as short-term use of a tranquilliser or beta-blocker (see Chapter 2) can sometimes be a possibility to see you through a difficult time, such as a funeral or a court appearance, or any situation which you find extremely stressful.

SELF-TALK
Pay attention to your thoughts, and look out for 'negative self-talk' in the days or weeks beforehand, such as 'I'll make a fool of myself ' or 'I can't do this'. This builds your anxiety and increases your self-doubt (see Chapter 7).

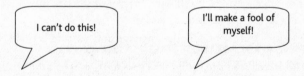

Replace such self-talk with positive and realistic thoughts such as 'If I prepare well, I can manage this', or, 'I have good skills, I can do this', or 'I'm quite good at this, I can get through it'.

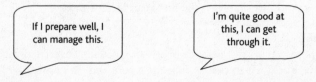

Assertiveness

Being assertive gives a solid foundation for coping with stressful situations where you have to communicate with others. We covered this is detail in Chapter 7, and everything you learned there will help you deal more effectively with other people, whatever the circumstances, from your partner to your child's teacher at parents' evening.

Here to remind you, are the main ideas which underpin assertiveness.

▶ Know your own needs and what you want.

▶ Acknowledge your own strengths and weaknesses.

▶ Have genuine respect for yourself and for others too.

▶ Be open, direct and honest whenever appropriate, and open to compromise.

And here are just a few of the skills which can be useful:

▶ Remember your rights as a human being. We're all just people.

▶ Keep your attitude pleasant, warm, and friendly.

▶ Smile a little if it feels right – it will give you an endorphin boost too!

▶ Speak fairly slowly, calmly and clearly, with warmth in your voice.

▶ An open and friendly body language and posture is best

▶ Don't be distracted from your main points – come back to them if you are.

Use assertiveness techniques such as:

▶ Asking for information

▶ Being specific

▶ Repeat a point calmly and warmly, if you feel it hasn't got across

▶ Accepting fair criticism

▶ Responding to unfair criticism

▶ Be ready to say 'no' if appropriate.

IMAGINE AHEAD

An excellent tool for stressful situations is 'visualization'. This has an unexpectedly powerful ability to reduce anxiety and stress about a forthcoming event. It can also have a positive effect on how things go on the day. My take on it is that dealing with it in your mind in advance takes the sting out of the anxiety you feel beforehand, and makes it all very familiar when the day arrives. It's as if you've 'been there and done that' many times already, but in a relaxed way, so there are fewer stressful associations.

So, as soon as you feel anxious, or for the week before, whichever is sooner, practise visualizing *every day*. For simplicity, let's call whatever it is you're planning to do, an 'event'. Start by practising Stage one, and then move on to Stage two when you're ready.

▶ **Stage one visualization**

Using a method which suits you, relax your whole body and mind for about two minutes.

Now, close your eyes and visualize the entire event as clearly as you can. Visualize every step, frame by frame like a video, from getting ready, to how you'll get there, to what happens during and after the event, and so on. Visualize everything going well, with no problems. Spend about 10–15 minutes on this.

When you are able to complete the entire visualization, you are ready to start to visualize in a different way, and move on to Stage two.

▶ **Stage two visualization**

Make a list of all the things which realistically may go wrong on the day. Just the ordinary everyday things, which happen all the time.

Now beside each, note down how you would best cope if that happened. Take time to think this through, now, rather than being surprised by it on the day.

Then prepare to visualize as in Stage one – using a method which suits you, relax your whole body and mind for about two minutes.

Then take the items from your list, one at a time, and visualize this going wrong, and you dealing with it calmly and appropriately in the way you've chosen. Use your quick relaxation method to reduce any anxiety this arouses.

Remember this

Key things to remember when visualizing are:

* Create a video in your mind's eye of what's going to happen. Make this as clear as you can manage, and go through it frame by frame.
* Visualize in as much detail as you can: colours, sights, sounds, speech and so on
* Whenever you feel any stress or anxiety coming on, press the pause button briefly, and use a quick method of relaxing to reduce that anxiety. When the level of anxiety falls continue with the visualization.

Coping with people in authority

Complaining in a shop or restaurant, a meeting with the bank manager or accountant, an interview at the Job Centre, school parents' evening, or even going to the doctor can feel like a challenge for many people. Dealing with authority figures can be particularly daunting or even intimidating, and is a common difficulty.

In addition to everything covered in the book so far, and reviewed at the beginning of this chapter, here is some specific know-how which can make situations like these less stressful:

► If you can, and it would help, take someone you trust with you for support.

- It's an old idea, but it still works – imagine the authority person in a funny outfit, or wearing underwear, or swim wear, or even naked, or on the toilet – this helps to make them seem more human, and on a more equal footing with you! The slight element of humour attached to this can also produce endorphins in the brain and makes you relax and feel better.

- Do a bit of research, so you know what you're about, and have your questions ready. Note them down in advance. And don't be afraid to have some notes with you – the authority person will probably have some, so you can too.

- Check out your rights in the particular situation.

- Be prepared to ask to see the manager or next person in the hierarchy, if necessary. No need to do this angrily, or forcefully. Just ask in a calm, assured voice.

INTERVIEW SKILLS

If an interview doesn't make you nervous, it shows you don't care enough about the job. Interviews make everyone nervous if they really want the job. Even the interviewers can be nervous sometimes. There is usually so much riding on them, and mostly, you've no idea what you might be asked. Nowadays you often have to come with a short talk or presentation already prepared to deliver on the day. All of this encourages stress.

Remember this

Take a second before you go into the interview room, to put on your confident body language. Then, open the door, and walk in confidently, even if you don't feel it. Walk tall, but relaxed. Shoulders relaxed, head up. Flash a smile at the interviewers. That will warm them to you, and give you an endorphin boost. Shake hands firmly when introduced.

In addition to your basic stress management skills, here are some hints and tips for interviews:

- Most importantly, *be prepared*. Make a list of the questions you might be asked, and prepare answers.

- Don't have alcohol or very spicy foods the night before (and on the day!), as your breath can give a very bad impression.

- Get to the interview half an hour early if you can. That way, your nerves will have time to settle. This also allows for transport hiccups, and time to freshen up, and to find a quiet spot to use a relaxation technique.

- Make sure you have eaten sensibly and healthily during the day before the interview. Low blood sugar makes you nervy, and it's difficult to concentrate (see Chapter 4).

- If you are shown around by a member of staff, they are often asked for their opinion of you afterwards. Stay relaxed and focussed, show real interest, and make relevant, sensible comments. You can plan these in advance.

- Request a glass of water before you start, if you feel you may dry up during the interview – or bring this in with you. Stress will dry your mouth.

- Politely decline the coffee or the biscuits. Stress can give you shaky hands, and talking and eating at the same time isn't easy.

- When you take a seat, keep your posture upright, but open and relaxed.

- Wear something appropriate and comfortable If it's new, try it out in advance to check for any unforeseen wardrobe malfunctions.

- Have your notes with you – the interviewer/s will have some, so you can too.

- As before, imagine the interviewers are in their underwear, or nude, or on the toilet.

- The first and last impressions that you make are the strongest – so pay particular attention to the start and end of your interview.

- End by thanking the interviewers for seeing you, and say why you really want the job. Make this only a sentence or two, and prepare it in advance.

EXAMS OR TESTS

Having been involved in education of various kinds for many years, I know that people aren't put forward for an exam or test if they don't have the ability to do it. So, the most important thing to do is believe in yourself. Therefore, if you just make sure to prepare properly, things should go well.

But don't try to be perfect. Aim to do your best but recognize that none of us can be perfect all of the time. There are so many people, who start revising for an exam with a score of 100% as their aim. They may not be aware that they are doing this, but think about it. When you revise, are you trying to know absolutely everything you might need to know? Are you making sure you can answer, any question or task that you're presented with, and do this really, really well?

It's great to succeed and reach for the stars. But keep things in balance. If you think that 'anything less than A++ means I've failed' then you are creating mountains of unnecessary work, and stress for yourself. For most exams, apart from tests for driving and similar skills, a score of 50, and sometimes 40, is a pass, and 65 is a pretty good pass. So you can actually afford not to know 35% of the answers, and still get a good pass. Exams are set to challenge the most able pupils, and give a good spread of marks for grading purposes, so something near to 100% of those taking the exam *will not* score 100%, and are not intended to. That's why pass marks can seem low.

It's not that you shouldn't have that A++ in your sights, it's just that when you're revising you can cut yourself a bit of slack, especially if a bare pass will do.

Long before the exam is on the horizon, you can do a lot to make passing easier. If you have a problem with the course work, do something about it straight away. Don't wait and worry. You can be sure it won't just be you. Ask another student, or the tutor. That's why you have a tutor or teacher. If you don't know how to prepare for the exam, getting stressed out won't help. Remember the NLP idea of focussing on solutions not problems, so take action to address the problem directly by seeing your course tutor straight away. Don't keep things bottled up. Keep things in perspective. The exam might seem like the most crucial thing in your life right now, but in the bigger picture of your whole life it's only a small part.

Tips for the revision or preparation period:

▶ Listen to all the advice from the tutor. Every exam or test is different, and the tutor will explain clearly what to expect, and how best to prepare.

▶ Avoid last minute cramming. Start in good time. This helps to boost your confidence and reduce stress, as you will know you have prepared well.

▶ Avoid the temptation to drink too much coffee, tea or fizzy drinks, which will overstimulate you making it harder to settle to your studies.

▶ Eat healthily and regularly. Regular moderate exercise will boost your energy, clear your mind and help you to relax. It's important to keep both body and mind in top gear, and keep your immune system spruced up. Easier to take it all in your stride too.

▶ Each day, use a relaxation technique, either one or two long sessions, or shorter sessions. You'll feel calmer and more balanced, with good concentration levels.

▶ When your mind loses concentration, take a short break. Five or ten minutes, or longer if you can. A walk in the fresh air, read a magazine or have a chat with friends, and you'll return to your revision refreshed.

▶ Try different revision techniques so that revision is more fun and your motivation stays high. Revise with friends if that helps.

Remember this

Make up a timetable so that you can see where you are with your revision, but allow time for fun and relaxation too, so that you come fresh to your studies each time, and avoid burning out before the exam.

Tips for the exam or test itself:

▶ Allow lots of time to get there, and arrive early to let your nerves settle, and freshen up in preparation for two or three hours in the exam room. Don't get sucked into 'worry and panic' chat with other students. Do some relaxation while you're waiting to go in.

▶ Remember all the necessary equipment and paperwork – check in advance what you'll need, and have a checklist to tick off if that helps.

▶ Take a few minutes to read the question paper through if there is a choice of questions. Then decide which you'll tackle.

▶ Work out the time allocation for each question, and stick to it. Not completing the correct number of questions is a very common reason for failing. So keep your eye on the clock.

▶ If there's a choice, start with an answer you are most confident about.

▶ If you feel yourself panicking, take a slow deep breath in, then sigh it out slowly, allowing your shoulders to relax, then use a relaxation technique to relax further.

After the exam is over, don't criticize yourself endlessly for where you think you went wrong. You will probably be wrong, and probably too harsh in your judgement. And remember you can mess up or miss out 50% and still pass on most exams. Congratulate yourself for all the planning and revision, and for getting through the exam. Focus on what you got right, and learn from the rest for next time.

Remember this

It's natural for your mind to go blank or lose concentration at some point. This happens to everyone, and can happen in any situation. Don't let this throw you. Just notice it has happened and go on to something else. Just like with meditation or mindfulness. Your mind will be back on track before you know it, if you don't react to it.

MAKING A PRESENTATION, SPEECH OR SHORT TALK

Just speaking to a group of two or three can make many people stressed. The sound of your own voice can be the strangest thing in the world, if you're not used to it. So sing in the shower, talk to your pet, recite nursery rhymes in the bath, give yourself a pep talk in the mirror, whatever makes your own voice more familiar.

If you can, it's best to start with something small, and do this a few times until you're confident with it, then move up a stage, practice at that level a few times, then move up to the next stage and so on.

As with the other situations, here are some suggestions to help make this kind of thing easier, teamed with the stress management skills covered throughout the book:

▶ Use a method of relaxing quickly, when you are waiting to start, and at any time you feel stressed.

▶ Don't tell your audience that you're not very good at public speaking, or that you're nervous. This reduces their confidence in you, and they can feel a bit nervous too. You'll pick up on this, and think you're messing up, making you more anxious so that you perform less well – a self-fulfilling prophecy.

▶ Be well prepared, have a checklist of what you need to take with you. Do some practice runs through, but not too many as you will become too familiar with it.

▶ Get there in good time, so that you can find the room, check any required equipment is there, set the chairs the way you want them, and get everything set out to make things go smoothly.

Lastly, keep in mind that this doesn't have to be perfect, stunning, and something they'll talk about for years to come. That's all in your head, putting unnecessary pressure on you. You just need to do a fair and reasonable job on this. Beyond that will be a bonus, and will come as your confidence builds.

Focus points

1. Everything you learn about stress management in this book can be applied to any stressful situation.

2. There is also special 'know-how' for most common stressful situations. If you can learn a bit about this too, as well as using stress management skills, you'll cope far better in any situation.

3. Visualizing a situation in all its detail beforehand, can considerably reduce feelings of stress and anxiety on the day.

4. Stress at work is very common, and has many different causes. But there is so much you can do about it.

5. Keeping your Personal Journal will help you move forward at a pace that suits you, and gets your priorities right.

13

User-friendly ways technology can help

Technology is part of everything we do, and managing stress is no different. Until now, technology has not had a major part to play in this book. This chapter will put that right by exploring how the internet, computer software and other technology can be used to assist with the stress management process. All of this is complementary material to dip into for those who are interested and comfortable with these media.

Making the most of the internet and modern technology

This is a field which is growing fast, and there's lots out there to use, much of it free, or relatively inexpensive to download from the internet, or use on-line. For a few pounds, you can have hi-tech ways of relaxing or managing stress. A few more pounds to spend and the choice and selection expands still more. There are also numerous types of instruments or monitors which can be used to learn to relax, with no need for a computer, CD or DVD.

How do you feel?

Here are five key ideas from this chapter to think about now. They will be discussed later:

1 How comfortable do you feel about using a computer to help you with your stress?

a Don't know

b Very comfortable

c Quite comfortable

d Uncomfortable

e Very uncomfortable

2 How comfortable do you feel about using technological gadgets to help you with your stress?

a Don't know

b Very comfortable

c Quite comfortable

d Uncomfortable

e Very uncomfortable

3 Which of these have you used to assess how stressed you are? (Choose all that apply.)

   a Stress dots

   b Stress card

   c Computer programme

   d Temperature sensor

   e None of these

   f Other

4 Do you currently spend time (choose all that apply):

   a On social networking sites

   b Playing computer/on-line games

   c Talking to friends/family on Skype

   d Blogging

   e Tweeting

   f E-mailing friends/family

   g Texting friends/family

   h None of these

5 Have you ever used biofeedback of any kind to help cope with stress?

   a Yes

   b No, never heard of it.

Mythbuster: You have to be technologically minded to use computers and gadgets

Computers, the internet and any gadgets relating to stress are all very user friendly nowadays. All that stops people is lack of confidence. If you can drive a car, turn on a radio, use a vacuum cleaner or food processer, you can use a computer and the internet.

Technology and the health service*

In all areas of the UK, the NHS has a detailed and comprehensive website for the public, with numerous other offshoots, which provide extensive specialist information, and diagnosis opportunities, and the option of speaking to someone for advice. The starting point for this is:

► www.nhsdirect.nhs.uk (UK wide)

► www.nhs24.com (Scotland)

Depending on where you live, and the interests and specialisms of nearby GPs and other health professionals, one or more of these may also be on offer:

► Special software programmes pre-loaded into terminals which you can use while you're at your surgery. These are actually effective computerized treatment programmes which you use over a number of sessions, offering effective stress and anxiety management, along with written information to take home with you.

► A terminal with access to on-line NHS information.

► Other special websites (see Optional extras).

► The use of a 24-hour heart rate/BP monitor if you're worried about how stress might be affecting your health over each day, and in the long term.

Technology and voluntary groups*

Numerous charities and voluntary groups have an established on-line presence with resources and support for stress and related difficulties. There is information to read or download, audio and video resources, discussion groups, and access to an on-line adviser. National organizations are available anywhere, but if you run a search you'll usually also find local and community level organizations too.

What is biofeedback?*

Relaxation is a fundamental part of managing stress, but it is a very individual thing, and for some stressed people, the techniques covered so far are just not for them. A useful alternative is to use biofeedback.

> ## Remember this
>
> There are various forms of biofeedback, but they all use the same principle of giving some form of immediate 'biological feedback' to a person, as to whether they are relaxing or not. This can be feedback on skin temperature, breathing or heart rate, or brain, muscle or skin activity.

The simplest form of biofeedback is probably stress dots, or 'biodots', a small self-adhesive, temperature sensitive disc, which you place on your wrist or forehead, and it changes colour in response to increasing or decreasing stress. High stress is shown by yellow, amber or black; low stress by turquoise or blue. This can also be done with small plastic strips, or cards similar to a credit card which you place a finger on. A simple temperature sensor can be attached to the skin, as skin temperature lowers and rises with stress, as blood is taken away from the extremities and the body surface to protect the core at times of physical threat.

Biofeedback monitors range from the very basic, to the elaborate and complex, but they mainly work on the same principle of monitoring a physiological measure which varies with stress. Many 'biofeedback' devices or monitors use feedback on 'galvanic skin response' or in other words how well your skin conducts electricity, as a measure of your stress level. This GSR increases with stress, due to increased sweating, and decreases as you relax. So a simple sensor attached to the fingers can be used to measure how well your skin is conducting electricity, and this can be converted to an audible tone, a light, or to a pointer, and this is a basic biofeedback monitor. As you relax the tone, light or pointer will fall or reduce to zero, giving immediate feedback that your efforts to relax are working, and encouraging you to continue. This can be very effective, and many people prefer this method of learning to relax, and enjoy seeing the pointer fall, or the light dim. Men tend to find this a good way to teach themselves to relax.

Specialist suppliers sell these at varying cost, some relatively inexpensive, and others right across the price range. Various computerized versions of biofeedback are also now available. Some are 'executive toys' using the output to run a toy car or train.

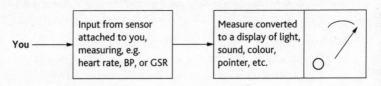

Biofeedback process

More technically advanced biofeedback monitors are coming on the market all the time, perhaps monitoring more bio-signs, such as blood pressure and heart rate, which rise with stress. Most simply require a couple of sensors to be attached using Velcro or other fixative. Alternatively, you simply need to place your fingers on to contacts, or some come in a watch-like monitor for the wrist, rather like those used by athletes to ensure they are working out effectively.

Other non-computer based equipment*

Not all technological developments make use of a computer, and current technology has much to offer on its own for managing stress:

▶ Make your own relaxing audio or visual material

It's so easy to make recordings. Using an iPod or MP3 player or a combined MP3/mobile phone, or similar, you can record or play any relaxing audio material you have, or make your own recording of whatever you find relaxing. This might be your own voice, or someone else's with helpful or encouraging thoughts or material, or you can talk yourself through a relaxation session. Most mobile phones and digital cameras will also easily record a short video, with sound. Video recorders are easy to use and not expensive. The only limit is your imagination.

▶ 'Light and sound' glasses

These are devices in the form of a headset, made up of a pair of special glasses and a set of headphones. They are designed to create relaxation and a calm mood through the use of sound and light patterns. These are microprocessor controlled devices. Just make your selection, put on the headphones and glasses, and sit back and relax.

Remember this

Contact information*

Throughout this chapter the various websites, equipment and software will be discussed in general terms only. Specific contact details and recommended sites will be given in Appendix 2. This kind of information changes almost by the second, so don't be put off if you have any difficulties accessing some of these sites, or finding what you are looking for. Just use your 'Search' facility to track down what you're looking for.

Think before you click

The World Wide Web is a fantastic resource with countless uses, but it pays to be careful with it, just as you would with any other new medium. Here are some thoughts:

▶ Only use reputable sites you are completely sure of.

▶ Don't give personal or financial information to anyone you cannot trust completely.

- Close down all windows which include personal or financial information, or password details, before leaving the computer – especially if using an internet café, library, or shared computer.

- Make sure you have anti-virus and firewall software fitted, and keep these up-to-date – new viruses and other threats appear every day.

- If you're unsure or in doubt at any time, it's best not to take any chances.

- Listen to your intuition. If it's telling you to tread warily, it's usually right.

Social networking sites like Facebook, Twitter or LinkedIn do have drawbacks, which you may well have heard about more than about the sites themselves. Identity theft is always a risk when you give information about yourself. So keep your wits about you, only use well-known and secure sites, and don't take any risks – it's just not worth it.

Free relaxing images and sounds*

The internet is a massive resource and source of information and downloadable audio and video material about all aspects of stress. Here is just a small taster of what you can find *free* on the web:

- Relaxing audio teamed with ever-changing tranquil pictures. Typical examples are the rainforest and birdsong, through to a purring cat, roaring ocean, sensational waterfalls, crackling log fire, whale sounds, the rhythmic sound of a train on a track. There is even the sound of a vacuum cleaner, for those with a baby who can only sleep when the vacuum is on.

- Soothing screensavers and peaceful pictures for your laptop or phone.

- Sensational sunsets, lakes, the northern lights, flowers, towering mountains.

- Plants, animals, landscapes, particular countries in the world, or parts of the UK.

- Night scenes, day scenes, from all parts of the globe.

- Audio and video downloads on time management, relaxation, meditation, mindfulness, and lots more.

Podcasts on the internet*

A podcast is a bit like a radio or TV show, which has a series of individual episodes that you can tune into. The difference is that the podcast is on the internet, not a TV, and is available any time, just like BBC iPlayer, ITV Player, and other TV channels, which let you watch and listen to channel programming when you want, not at set times.

Remember this

Podcasts are a great way to access more substantial amounts of material, such as information, sounds, pictures and video (sometimes called 'vidcasts' or 'video podcasts') on the net.

You can either watch or listen to the podcast on-line, or download it onto a computer, or whichever equipment you prefer. It's easy to find vast assortments of material which you can download covering relaxation, tension, stress and related topics, most of it of high quality, and much of it free. A few pounds will open the door to still more.

Biofeedback software*

Biofeedback was introduced earlier, and as its name suggests is about a person being given some kind of feedback, as to whether they are relaxing or not, based on a biological or physiological measure. So, as you relax you'll receive immediate feedback that it is working, and this encourages you to continue.

There is a growing range of software available, which allows you to learn and practise biofeedback techniques, level by level, as you take in breath-taking three-dimensional landscapes, soothing music, and inspiring visuals, or play carefully constructed games. Your physiological responses are measured using a simple monitor, which comes with the software, and this information is fed continuously into the computer. Most come with their own training manual with tips and strategies for different biofeedback methods as you search for precious stones, play mental games, solve puzzles, land an air balloon or helicopter, and all of that kind of thing.

Biofeedback like this can be surprisingly effective, and many people enjoy this way of learning to relax and taking their mind off stress too. There are many websites devoted to biofeedback on the internet, and a simple search should guide you towards detailed explanation about how it works, along with practical advice about how to use different types of biofeedback.

Social networking sites*

Socializing with other people is vital to our health and wellbeing. The 'social support' this brings is an essential part of our resilience and cushioning from stress. Preferably this would be in the real world, but a useful alternative these days can be the social networking site (SNS). In the business world, networking sites are becoming a key part of meeting and keeping new clients, and keeping in touch with colleagues. Many people have their favourite SNS as their home page on their computer, checking it every day for what's new and who's doing what. We now glory in news of the inconsequential. And there's nothing wrong with that. It's a good way to take your mind off everyday stressors. This makes a change from all the major stresses we face every day in our real world, and delivers social support instantly and in spades. Provided you're careful (see earlier section 'Think before you Click'), SNSs have great potential for reducing stress.

Case study

Aisha had just moved to a new area as she'd had the step up she had been working so hard for at work, and was transferring to another branch. It was bad timing though, as she'd just split up with long-term boyfriend, Rafi. It was hard leaving family and friends, and settling in to her new job was harder than she expected, so she was feeling quite stressed about it all, and missed having her friends around to sound off to in the evenings. Shopping on the net one weekend, she found herself signing up to a social networking site for the first time. The next evening, there was a message in from an old school friend, Melissa, who was living only a few streets away from her! She was also soon in contact with other people she knew in the area, and feeling much better.

PRIVACY ON SNSs

You'll find specific privacy settings for photos, messages, each part of your profile and so on, and it's crucial you attend to this. You can choose who will and who won't see your material. You can block individuals you don't want knowing you exist on the particular SNS, and you can create a 'Limited Profile' to hide certain parts of your profile from specific friends. But you have to set this up, the 'default' for many sites, is full public access.

Blogging*

The term 'weblog' was formed in 1999 by combining the words 'website' and 'logging', to describe ' logging' comments and links on your own website. 'Weblog' was then shortened to 'blog'. So opinions, pictures, and information of all kinds from ordinary people or celebrities can traverse the globe unbelievably quickly.

It's incredibly easy to create your own blog, or 'comment' on another person's. Blogging has been described as a very cathartic activity, which can aid relaxation, and help to combat stress. You can pour everything out into your own daily or weekly blog, safely releasing all the pent-up pressure, tension and the frustration of living. And you can generate discussion with those who 'comment' on your blog too. There are also *'blog rings'*, which are linked communities of bloggers who have a shared interest. So any stress-related topic should be covered and community support offered. These rings can be found via Technorati's blog finder (details in Optional extras). If you can't find exactly what you are looking for, you can even establish a blog ring for yourself.

Focus points

1. For those who want it, the internet is a wonderful source of helpful material and information, much of it free, and provides opportunities for networking, campaigning and on-line support.

2. Statutory services such as the NHS and the Health and Safety Executive have a broad-ranging and very useful on-line presence, as do many voluntary groups.

3. Technological advances continually produce a wide range of equipment and devices to aid stress management, including biofeedback indicators and monitors.

4. Software packages which allow various stress management activities, some with biofeedback built in, can be very effective, and enjoyable.

5. Social networking, blogging, podcasting and other on-line activities can be helpful in coping with stress, for some people.

How to stay on track – and twenty key habits to manage your stress

This last chapter will look at the following and how these relate to managing stress:

▶ *Being sure of your needs and priorities*
▶ *Ways to find the energy and keep working on managing your stress*
▶ *Where to go from here*
▶ *Twenty key ways to cope better with stress.*

Looking back, looking forward

Much has been covered since you made a start on this book, and it's good that you're still sticking with it to this last chapter, even if you're just skimming the book. Stress has been explained in all its aspects: what causes it, how it can make people feel, the kinds of people who are particularly likely to experience it, and what you can do to help yourself to cope better with it. And this is just a starting point from which you can continue to build, and learn more, and I hope I've encouraged you to do that, and broaden your horizons. There have been numerous possible jumping-off points, either in the main text, with subjects like NLP, mindfulness and biofeedback introduced, or from the Optional extras. Perhaps some topics haven't been of interest right now, but they may be of use in the weeks or months ahead, so keep this book to hand, to dip into if it's needed.

How do you feel?

For the final time, here are five key ideas from this chapter to think about now. They will be discussed later:

1 What do you think made you read this book? Try to put this into words.

2 At this moment, how *determined* are you to do something about your stress? Try scoring this on a scale of 0–100, 100 meaning you're as determined as it's possible to be.

3 How much *energy* do you feel you have to do something about your stress?

   a A little

   b Quite a lot

   c I'm totally drained

   d Hardly any

   e More than enough

   f Don't know

4 Have you made a start using any of the stress management techniques from this book? (Choose any that apply.)

    a I need time to think about it

    b I'm in two minds

    c I've already started a couple of things

    d Don't know

    e I'm using lots of the ideas and techniques

    f Not sure I can do it

    g I'm already improving.

5 Which of these people do you have on your side right now? (Choose all that apply.)

    a Partner

    b Friend/s

    c Family

    d Yourself

    e This book

    f Work colleague/s

    g Doctor

    h Boss

    i Don't know

    j Other

Keeping going

Just reading this book, and reaching this last chapter shows that you do really want to overcome your stress, so this is a great starting point for you to go on to accomplish what you set out to achieve. Sometimes it can all seem such an effort. But it is most definitely worth it.

Just as with everything else, you may have ups and downs along the way, but keep going, work on improving your overall health and wellbeing, in the various ways explained in this book (especially Chapters 3, 4, 5, 6, and 11) and your energy levels and motivation will increase, and you will get there.

Case study

Fatima

Fatima is a mother of two small children, living in a tent in a famine-stricken area of Africa. Her husband Kamal died on the way to the camp. She and the children shared one very small meal yesterday, but they are all hungry today, with nothing to eat so far.

▶ In your Journal, make a list of what you feel to be Fatima's most urgent needs.

▶ List what you feel might be her less urgent needs.

Chloe

Chloe is also a mother of two small children, but she is living on benefits in a high-rise council flat in London. Her partner Liam left her a year ago for someone else. She has enough food to last until her next benefit payment, but her doctor diagnosed depression yesterday, and she starts on medication for it today.

▶ List what you feel to be Chloe's most urgent needs.

▶ List what you feel might be her less urgent needs.

Now start a new page, and head it 'MY NEEDS'. Make a list of what you feel are *your* most urgent needs right now, today. Take time to think about it. That can be hard to work out, and everyone is different.

Needs like these lie at the heart of us all. They are what makes us behave as we do, what motivates us, and to some extent what makes us tick. But there is much more to it than we've touched on in this case study. Human needs come in many, many forms, and are hugely dependent on the life situation we find ourselves in, as is obvious from Chloe and Fatima's lives.

To feel 'contented' or even to feel happy, people must have certain needs met. Think again of Fatima in war-torn and famine-stricken Africa, and Chloe on a council estate in London. They are both mothers, but there the similarity ends. Their needs will be very different. One will be desperately worried about how she will find food for her children today, not to mention herself, and how she will protect them from real and threatening danger. The other may have enough to feed her children for the week, until the next benefit payment, and have the warmth and security of a council flat, but may be truly depressed as she feels she lacks self-respect because she has to rely on the state to feed her children. She may see no way forward, and have no sense of purpose.

Abraham Maslow (1908–70) saw human needs as a hierarchy, or ladder, in which the basic human bodily needs were on the bottom rung; safety needs came next, followed by higher order needs such as the desire for love, self-esteem or a sense of belonging. Only if the lower order needs such as hunger and safety are met, will people be concerned with meeting the higher order needs. So Fatima's mind was likely to be fully taken up with the lower order needs of food, shelter and safety for her children, as without them, they could all be dead within days. Chloe had these needs met, and so could concern herself with her higher order needs such as self-respect and respect from others, and possibly even higher needs – and this could have caused her depression.

Here is a sample of Maslow's hierarchy of needs, with needs ranked most urgent or lower order, first. The highest order need, to self-actualize, means to realize oneself to the fullest, to make real all of your potential, and to 'be all you can be'. This may well take a life-time to achieve. Many will never meet this need, and may never have the chance to even think about it, as they are entirely taken up with lower order needs throughout their lives.

```
Low order |  Food, drink

              Shelter

            To be loved

     To have a sense of belonging

            To be valued

         To respect oneself

       To be respected by others

     To have a sense of achievement

      To have a sense of purpose

High order |     To self-actualize
```

Here is Maslow's hierarchy of needs in more detail:

Maslow's hierarchy of needs in detail	
Bodily needs	Food, water, air, sex
Safety needs	Security, comfort, freedom from fear
Belongingness and love needs	Love, belongingness, affiliation
Esteem, respect needs	Competence, approval, recognition, self-respect, respect from others, being valued, achievement
Purpose needs	Long and short-term goals and direction
Thinking needs	Knowledge, understanding, novelty, intellectual stimulation
Artistic needs	Beauty, order, creativity
Self-actualization	Fulfilment, full potential realized.

What are your needs?

Try it now

Have a look back at the list of your own needs from the Case Study about Fatima and Chloe. Do any of these appear in Maslow's hierarchy, even in general terms?

Have a try at listing all of your needs once again, this time adding in anything you identify with from Maslow's needs. Try arranging them all in order, with most urgent first, and so on.

For each of this new list of needs, make a note of whether or not it is currently met, or if it isn't, how you might try to meet this need.

How does your second list of needs compare with your first?

Did you find doing this difficult or easy? For most people, this is a difficult exercise. You may have few needs, or you may have many. Or you may find putting ideas like these down on paper very demanding. You may not know where to start. For others this can be a releasing activity, allowing them at last to put into words the thoughts which have been floating around in their heads for some time.

Remember this

Maslow believed that the motivation for people's actions and behaviour arose from their needs. The more urgent or strong the need, the greater the motivation.

This short look at the topic of needs and motivation has illustrated that we are sometimes unaware of how our needs might be affecting us. This is not in any deep sense, such as unconscious or subconscious thoughts. It is simply in the sense that our everyday thinking and actions, including feeling stressed, may be influenced by underlying needs and aspirations of which we are unaware, tucked away at the back of our minds or in our hearts. And it is these unseen needs which may be driving and guiding our feelings, reactions and behaviour, to a greater or lesser extent.

Ten ways to keep to your new plans

1 You could tell someone you really trust about your plans – then they'll ask you about them. A kind of 'stress buddy'. Only do this if you're comfortable with it.

2 Out of sight is often out-of-mind where plans are concerned. So, use your Personal Journal as a guide, prompt, and reminder. If you like, you can write down what you plan to do in large brightly coloured print on a poster size sheet of paper, and display this prominently somewhere you can't miss it. For more private or confidential plans, write them on a card and keep them somewhere only you will see them.

3 You're much more likely to be successful if you have just one or two new things to concentrate on at a time. You are far more likely to stick to just one than if you have a whole list to work on at the same time. So take things one or two at a time, until these are established.

4 Recruit a friendly *mentor* or *supporter* to encourage you or badger you, whichever works for you! Your mentor can also be the person you call at that crisis point when you are desperately tempted to let things slip. So instead of reaching for the biscuit barrel, a drink, a cigarette or a chocolate bar – reach for the phone and your mentor will talk you out of it!

5 For the technologically minded, you could arrange for a 'pop-up' to appear on your PC or mobile phone or iPad to remind and encourage you. Something like: 'Remember you were going to jog twice a week – go on, you can do it!', or 'Time to do a quick relaxation session.'

6 You're also much more likely to stick to a plan which is realistic and do-able. So if you've slipped already, maybe you could adapt yours to be easier to actually achieve. You can always take the next step after you've managed the first more realistic one, and then the next, and so on. So if you've decided you'll take the children out every week, and have already failed miserably, how about aiming for once a fortnight?

7 You can also write down the benefits you (or others) will gain from your plans. Read these regularly, and especially when tempted to give up.

8 Set yourself actual targets, rather than having vague general aims. 'I'll sign up for that Zumba class at the community centre by the end of June', not 'I'll start going to Zumba somewhere, soon'.

9 'Carrot and stick' is often a key with plans. Having both is often the most effective way to ensure you stick to your plan! So set clear targets, and if achieved, choose an appropriate reward for yourself, such as that expensive magazine you've had your eye on. But equally, if you don't achieve your target, decide in advance a suitable task for yourself which you would really rather not have to do, like tidying that drawer which you've been avoiding for weeks.

10 Review your progress regularly, at the same time every week, when you know you'll have time.

Mythbuster

Managing stress is not rocket science. It's a range of very straightforward techniques and ideas. It's all about knowing how, and finding the heart and the energy to do something about it.

Sort out your priorities

The priorities of life and how to choose them and remember them has been touched on throughout the book, especially when lifestyle, resilience, work/life balance, NLP and healthy thinking were being discussed. We can pick up again on this now.

When dealing with stress, it can be useful to consider the bigger issues in life, and how important these are to you. This is a key part of your identity, and one which very much can make you who you are, and influence many of the more important decisions and choices you make in life.

Work your way through the following list, marking each item with the number which best fits how you would currently rate how important that item is to you:

This does not matter to me at all	Not so important to me	Quite important to me	Very important to me	Extremely important to me
0	1	2	3	4

Don't agonize too much on the answers; your first thought is likely to be nearest the truth.

Make a note in your Journal if there are any others you would like to add, along with their rating.

Rate each according to how important you feel each item is to you, in general, most of the time.

Add anything you feel is missing.

Subject area	Rating	Subject area	Rating
HELPING OTHERS		HAVING A PARTNER	
INDEPENDENCE		FRIENDS	
LEARNING		ADVENTURE	
VARIETY		TO LOVE	
NOVELTY		MARRIAGE	
WORK/CAREER		POWER	
CHALLENGE		PASSION	
APPROVAL		INTEGRITY	
LEADERSHIP		SUCCESS	
HAPPINESS		FREEDOM	
INTIMACY		RESPECTED	
YOUR HOME		ACHIEVEMENT	
SECURITY		EXCITEMENT	
AFFECTION		MONEY	
PHYSICAL FITNESS		HEALTH	
STATUS		TRAVEL	
HAVING CHILDREN		YOUR FAMILY	
ACADEMIC ACHIEVEMENT		ARTISTIC ACHIEVEMENT	
ACHIEVEMENT IN SPORT		PHYSICAL ACHIEVEMENT	
SPIRITUALITY		PEACE OF MIND	
TO BE LOVED		OTHER?	

When you've finished, take a new page in your Journal, and head it, PRIORITIES. Then note there, down the left-hand side of the page, your five highest scoring items, in order, highest first.

▶ Do these surprise you at all? YES/NO

▶ In terms of these five items and any other high-scoring items, does your life currently allow you to meet all of these needs? YES/NO

▶ If NO, think about how you might go about meeting these needs, and make a note of this opposite each item. Include any others you want.

Enter these new plans into the section of your Journal, in your *now, soon* or *later* lists.

Mythbuster: People who are stressed just need to pull themselves together

Pulling yourself together, whatever that means, will only make things worse, as it gives an impression of increasing the physical and mental tension that's already there. The opposite is actually true. Stressed people need to let go, and relax their body and mind.

Twenty key habits of people who cope well with stress

People who cope well with stress:

1 Think about whether the cause of their stress can be removed or reduced, and do something about it, if it's possible.

2 Cushion themselves from stress and build resilience against stress.

3 Avoid hurry and rushing.

4 Can look confident even if they don't feel it.

5 Take regular breaks, and get a good night's sleep.

6 Are nice to themselves, and have 'me-time'.

7 Accept offers of help when they want to.

8 Sort out their priorities, and are organized – they know where they are, where they want to go, and how they plan to get there.

9 Respect their own needs and those of others, know how to compromise, and can say no when they want to.

10 Make time for enjoyable pastimes, keep fit and take enjoyable exercise.

11 Find a trusted friend to talk to and share things with. Have friends who are positive, up-beat, and supportive.

12 Eat healthily avoid too much caffeine, and don't skip meals.

13 Focus on solutions, not problems.

14 Don't use alcohol or non-prescription drugs to combat stress.

15 Think healthily and positively. Smile and laugh often.

16 Pay attention to other people's use of words, and body language, and communicate well with them.

17 Use mindfulness at some point every day.

18 Check their breathing regularly – and if it's too fast, slow this down, and use their tummy, not their upper chest to breathe.

19 Scan their body for stress and tension regularly each day.

20 Relax mind and body completely for at least ten minutes every day.

You can do it!

Stick at it. Overcoming your stress is within your grasp, right there, just in touching distance, so you must go for it. It will take a little time and effort. But it will be worth it. You can overcome your stress and it will be a huge relief. When you suddenly notice that you aren't having to make an effort any more, and it's weeks since you felt stressed, you will know you *have* overcome your stress. Your life will have become more relaxed and more comfortable, and 'back to normal' and that is certainly worth working for. That is something to achieve, something to look forward to. So follow the guidance in this book. *Make* it work. You can do that.

Remember this

Your Personal Journal

Continue to keep the Personal Journal you began in Chapter 4 up to date, with your daily stress scores, brief description of each week, and your three lists of changes and new techniques you plan to implement *now*, *soon*, or *later*, and continue moving these forward. When the time is right, move items in *soon*, into *now*, and those from *later* into *soon*...and so on. And this doesn't need to be just for stress-related items. You can start using this system for your other plans too.

Focus points

Consider the points below and record your thoughts in your Personal Journal.

1. What are the *main* causes of your stress right now?
2. What are your *most common* symptoms of stress right now?
3. What are the five most useful things you've learned from this book?
4. What do you think will help to *motivate* you to keep working on your stress tomorrow, the next day, and in the coming weeks?
5. What are you going to do tomorrow towards overcoming your stress?

Optional extras:

Appendix 1

This appendix contains optional activities you can work on or follow up if you want to. They are listed chapter by chapter. These might be case studies to read, or techniques and activities to try.

Website and contact details are given in Appendix 2.

► **Some more signs and symptoms of stress**
Physical:

- ► headaches
- ► indigestion
- ► churning stomach
- ► palpitations
- ► difficulty taking a deep breath
- ► difficulty swallowing
- ► tingling of hands or feet
- ► nausea
- ► fatigue
- ► aches and pains
- ► muscle twitches
- ► sweating
- ► muscle tension
- ► weight gain or loss
- ► trembling
- ► dry mouth

- insomnia
- poor balance
- hyperventilation.

Mind:
- anxiety
- worry
- depression
- panic attacks
- negative outlook
- hopelessness
- fearfulness
- gloomy thoughts
- poor concentration
- withdrawal
- feelings of unreality
- feelings of depersonalization
- feeling unable to cope.

Behaviour:
- restlessness
- agitation
- making mistakes
- forgetfulness
- violent outbursts
- change in usual behaviour

- pacing up and down, or round about
- hand-wringing
- indecision
- anger
- shouting
- irritability
- aggression
- eating too much or too little
- inability to cope
- increased substance use
- avoiding difficult situations.

CHAPTER 1

Case studies

Linda, from Shropshire

Linda is 42, single and very much enjoys her own company in her small house, which she has arranged just as she likes it. She has relatives staying with her from Australia, a cousin she hasn't seen for ten years, and his wife and two noisy small children. They have already been with her for three weeks and there's another two to go. This week, whilst doing the weekly shop, she suddenly felt a feeling of acute panic, palpitations, light-headedness and nausea.

Comment:

Linda is clearly someone who has experienced a panic attack as a result of the fight or flight response being triggered whilst thinking about her overcrowded house, and another week's meals, snacks and drinks to plan for – a short-term problem. Her relatives will soon depart and hopefully all should be well again. But she would be well advised to learn how to manage short-term stress better for the future.

Michael, from Rotherham

Michael took his driving test for the second time today, and failed. He is 22 and had taken lots of lessons to practise for this road driving part of the test, but he couldn't control his nerves and had made several serious mistakes.

Comment:

Michael has not passed his road driving test because his ANS arousal was too high for the job in hand, probably because of the psychological threat of a second failure. He will need to learn how to manage his stress next time.

CHAPTER 2

Case studies

Evening surgery in Manchester:

Alexander, 47 years

Alexander comes into the doctor's consulting room slowly. He avoids eye contact and appears agitated. With some prompting, he explains that he is tired all the time. He is totally exhausted. He goes to bed early, sometimes at nine o'clock, and sleeps all night but he is still tired and drained. Things have got so bad that he can no longer cope and something will have to be done because he's certain something is seriously wrong. His tiredness has taken over his life, taking over everything. The doctor finds his manner difficult and it's almost as if he is angry with the whole world.

Diagnosis after discussion and tests: Tired all the time (TATT) caused by stress.

Hannah, 29

Hannah knows she isn't coping with life very well. She tells the doctor she's is extremely worried about her coming marriage as she isn't sure that it's the right thing to do. She feels that she is under a lot of parental pressure to marry her boyfriend, but she isn't sure. She is losing sleep and has had a warning at work for making silly mistakes. She is also suffering from tummy cramps and her tummy is often grossly swollen. She can hardly get into her trousers. Sometimes, she's constipated, but other times she gets diarrhoea, so she never knows where she is.

Diagnosis after discussion and tests: Irritable Bowel Syndrome with intestinal colic, contributed to by stress.

Gary, 23

Gary has begun to avoid eating with his family. He's worried in case his hand shakes. One day, a few months ago, his hand shook when he was writing something at work, when his new line manager, who is a perfectionist, and gets annoyed about mistakes, was watching him. Gary was incredibly embarrassed, and is avoiding having to do that again. Then a week or two later, his hand shook when he was drinking with his friends, so now he avoids outings with his friends in case it happens again and they laugh at him. He is now so scared of his hand shaking, that the fear has made it happen more often, reinforcing the belief that it's going to happen. He feels that he is going mad, and now won't go out anywhere his hand might shake.

Diagnosis after discussion and tests: Possibly the beginnings of a social phobia, contributed to by stress.

CHAPTER 3

Case studies

Some stressed people and their stories

Rona, 44, from Oxford

Rona rushes straight from work to her hairdresser, Angela, carrying two heavy bags of shopping and a soaked umbrella. She sits down uneasily. She looks agitated, and she's desperate for a cigarette.

'I'm living on my nerves these days, Angela', she says in reply to Angela asking how she is today. She continues almost without taking a breath,

'It's these two boys of mine. They fight all the time, and the oldest one has just been suspended from school for talking back to teachers. I can't do anything with him. He just says what am I going to do about it? He's nearly six feet, and I'm five feet two. He won't listen to Sasha either. He just says he's not his real dad, so he can't tell him what to do.'

John, 54, from Essex

John has recently had a role change at work. He didn't have much say in this, and he's finding adjusting to a new job harder than he used to. What with that and just having moved to a new flat, with a bigger mortgage, he's been feeling on edge a lot lately. He hardly hears from his two sons these days, as they had a bit of a falling-out when his marriage broke up, and he finds it very lonely. The other night, after he'd gone to bed, he heard someone trying to open his front door. He phoned the police, but they didn't come for hours, and when they did come, they didn't find anyone. That was three months ago, but he's not had a proper night's sleep since. He can't get to sleep for listening for noises, and when he does fall asleep he wakes up in a terrible panic.

Kathy, 25, from Edinburgh

Kathy lives in a run-down area of the city. She lives with the father of her seven-year-old son, and two-year-old daughter. She is just 25. Her mother looks after the children for her whenever she can to give her a break. Kathy is constantly exhausted and on edge, and tends to snap at the children. Her two-year-old, Maya, has frequent tantrums which seem to be getting worse, and seven-year-old Ben is bed-wetting every night. Her boyfriend has been unemployed since she met him, and leaves it all to her and goes out drinking every night.

CHAPTER 4

▶ **Mind and body – a vicious circle of stress**

An individual's mind and body interact in a complex way.

Case study

Barry, who is 49, has become so worried lately, that he isn't sleeping. In the past year, there have been so many changes in strategy and staffing in the chain store where he is the manager, he can hardly keep up with them. He's had to work late almost every night for over a month, to try to get back on top of it. When he eventually gets home he can't relax, and is sure he can feel his heart racing for no reason. In the mornings, he wakes up, still exhausted, and dreads going to work. In the past few days, he's noticed mild chest pain, now and then, at work. He's sure it's just indigestion, but inside he feels panicky and scared. Every day, things just seem to get worse, and he's thinking 'What if I have a heart attack?'

Comment: Barry finds himself in a vicious circle, becoming more and more anxious and afraid he has heart trouble. Barry is finding work very stressful, and this has caused his heart rate to rise, especially as he's let his fitness go. Worrying about his heart racing has increased his stress response, producing more symptoms, such as tense chest muscles, which adds more worry...and more stress...and so on. This process is very common, and very distressing if you are caught up in it. Similar fears can arise from many physical stress symptoms, but especially those connected with headaches, the heart, breathing and balance. The way out of the vicious circle is to see a doctor about any worrying symptoms.

CHAPTER 5

▶ **Rapid Relaxation Technique 2**

1 Follow the instructions as for Ten Steps Relaxation (Chapter 5), but speed up the whole process, so that you can complete it and become relaxed within a minute or two.

↓

2 Finish off as for Technique 1 (Chapter 5).

▶ **Rapid Relaxation Technique 3**

1 Lie or sit comfortably, allowing your breathing to become slow and regular.

↓

2 Now, all at the same time, deliberately tense up tightly *your whole body*, and hold it for a few seconds: hands, arms, shoulders, neck and head, face, back and stomach, legs and feet (as in Ten Steps Relaxation). Then suddenly, let it all go, and allow relaxation to take over.

↓

3 Repeat the whole process once more if necessary.

↓

4 Enjoy the relaxation for a few moments or minutes, then finish off your session as for Technique 1.

CHAPTER 6

▶ **More guided imagery**

Read over the scenarios described below. Choose one to work on today. You can make a recording of the description if that is easier.

When you're happy you know what to do, settle back somewhere comfortable and relax your body as much as possible, using any technique which works for you.

Then gently close your eyes, and begin to gradually develop a picture of yourself in your mind's eye, in ONE of the following settings, in as much detail and as vividly as you can. Use all your senses to see, feel, hear, smell and touch.

On a fluffy cloud:

Relaxing as you lie peacefully and comfortably on a warm white fluffy cloud...completely safe and at ease...high in a blue, blue sky...drifting slowly along in the gentle breeze...you feel the warmth of the sunshine...

Grass and forest:

Walking quietly, or lying totally at peace, on a grassy mountaintop...you can see the tropical forest far beneath you... the early morning rains just over...and feel the warmth of the newly risen orange sun...you can hear birdsong...and what can you touch with your outstretched fingertips?...can you feel the soft, moist, grass underfoot?...

By the sea:

Lying or sitting comfortably on the soft, warm sand, watching or just listening to the sea as the waves roll gently in...and... out, in...and...out.... Watch the movement, see the next wave coming, smell the sea air, feel the wetness of the spray, hear the seabirds...

Take as long as you like, then slowly let the image go, begin to pay attention to your breathing, and your surroundings. Allow yourself to become more and more alert, until you are fully aware and alert again.

▶ **Meditation**

More mantras:

Om mani padme hum (Tibetan – means *Hail the jewel in the lotus*)

Ra-mah

So-hum

Peace

So-ham

Relax

Ham…sa (place on your inward and outward breaths)

Ahnam.

More mandalas:

Picture or image of your choice, preferably involving circles

A sunflower head in full bloom

Ripples on a pond

A bird's nest with eggs inside.

CHAPTER 7

Assertiveness case studies

Anne, from Cardiff

Anne is a widow. She enjoys her part-time job in the local baker's shop and has just had her 55th birthday. She has one daughter and two grandchildren, and she is very fond of them all. She used to really enjoy looking after the two girls, aged four and seven for her daughter whenever she could. But lately her daughter has been taking her for granted assuming she will take care of the girls, often with no notice and even if she has other plans, and Anne just can't say no to her. Anne also does shopping and housework for an elderly neighbour, even though he has family of his own nearby. Recently Anne has been feeling completely drained, very tense, and starts at the slightest noise. She just can't seem to relax, and has developed neck and shoulder pain. She can't decide what to do.

Comment:

Anne just can't say no, and needs to learn how to do so, in a way that other people can accept. She will then take control of her workload, and be able to tailor it to her abilities.

Mark, from County Antrim

Mark is finding his job very stressful. He's 35 and works in a large high street shop, where he's just been promoted to supervise a number of sales assistants. He used to really enjoy his work, but he is finding it stressful now because none of the assistants like him, and they seem to go out of their way to annoy him. He feels depressed and can't think what he's done to upset them. He thinks it might have something to do with how he deals with them if they need to be pulled up for something. He just seems to make them angry, as he finds it difficult to criticize in a way which doesn't devalue them.

Comment:

If Mark can learn how to criticize constructively, and with respect, his work colleagues will begin to respect him and he will enjoy his work again.

CHAPTER 8

Case studies

Kenny and Laura: Panic and control

Kenny is finding it increasingly difficult to cope with the work on his course in microbiology at a large university. It's his first semester, and the lectures are complicated, and the pace much faster than he expected. It's difficult to get to know people as the lectures have so many people in them. He now feels after only six weeks, that the work is totally out of his control, and that he just isn't up to it. He's also been feeling panicky and light-headed during lectures, and has twice had to leave the lecture before the end. Why do these things always happen to him? Just his luck. He's sure he'll have to give up at the end of the semester, and is angry that life just isn't fair.

Comment: Kenny has an external locus of control. This means he feels he can't do anything to change his situation, as it's outside his control.

Laura is on the same microbiology course as Kenny. She found the sudden increase in pace and level a shock at first, but realized she would need to put in more study to keep up. Laura has noticed Kenny leaving lectures early, and wasn't sure what was wrong. Laura also made a point of talking to other students, to find out how they were coping with the course, and discovered they all felt the same. It was tough for them all. She finds the library really helpful for reading up on the parts of the book she finds difficult to understand, and the tutorials are very useful for asking questions. She's pretty sure she'll cope and is enjoying the new experience.

Comment: Laura has an internal locus of control. This means she feels she can do things to change her situation, as it's within her control.

CHAPTER 9

▶ Mindfulness Based Stress Reduction (MBSR)

Dr Jon Kabat-Zinn developed the Mindfulness Based Stress Reduction (MBSR) programme at the University of Massachusetts Medical Center in 1979. MBSR is now a form of complementary medicine addressing a variety of health problems including chronic pain and low self-esteem, as well as stress. Mindfulness Based Stress Reduction brings together mindfulness, meditation and yoga, and is delivered as eight weekly classes and one day-long class covering the following:

▶ guided instruction in mindfulness meditation practices

▶ gentle stretching and mindful yoga

▶ group dialogue and discussions aimed at enhancing awareness in everyday life

▶ individually tailored instruction

▶ daily home assignments

▶ four home practice CDs and a home practice manual.

▶ The Centre for Mindfulness Research and Practice

In the UK, the Centre for Mindfulness Research and Practice (CMRP) is a self-funding organization based in the School of Psychology at Bangor University. CMRP was the first organization in the UK to establish professional training in the field on mindfulness, and is committed to the promotion of wellbeing through the application of mindfulness-based approaches. The Centre is committed to integrity, scientific rigour, and excellence in teaching and research, and trains professionals in the application of mindfulness based approaches and researches applications of mindfulness. They also offer classes in mindfulness based stress reduction (MBSR) and mindfulness based cognitive therapy (MBCT) to professionals and the general public both locally and further afield.

▶ Mindfulness-based Cognitive Therapy (MBCT)

MBCT is an integration of MBSR with Cognitive Behaviour Therapy (CBT). It was developed to help people suffering from depression, and has been shown to help recovered recurrently depressed participants, through teaching them skills to disengage from habitual 'automatic' unhelpful cognitive patterns.

CHAPTER 10

See websites and contacts in Appendix 2.

CHAPTER 11

See websites and contacts in Appendix 2.

▶ Qigong

Qigong is a 5,000-year-old Chinese practice designed to promote the flow of 'chi', the vital life force that flows throughout the body, regulating its functions. Qigong (pronounced CHEE-gong) means 'the skill of attracting vital energy'. It is an ancient art which combines movement and meditation, and makes use of visualizations to strengthen the connection of body and mind. Regular practice can bring balance, and bring together mind, body and spirit.

▶ The scientific approach to acupuncture

It is still not clear exactly how acupuncture works, from a pragmatic and scientific point of view. Here are two suggestions:

1 Acupuncture may stimulate the secretion of endorphins in the body.

2 Neurotransmitter levels, such as serotonin may be affected by acupuncture.

▶ Emotional Freedom Technique

The Emotional Freedom Techniques (EFT) is a group of very simple processes which have been used to help people to cope with stress, anxiety, phobias, and for general confidence building. The founder of EFT is Gary Craig, and since its development in 1995, it has become enormously popular, with strong anecdotal support. The key process is to stimulate energy meridian points on your body by tapping on them with your fingertips. These points are to be found on the face, the hands, the head and the upper torso. Once learned, or shown to you, the process is easily remembered.

See www.tapping.com

CHAPTER 12
See websites and contacts in Appendix 2.

CHAPTER 13

▶ Some of the most popular social networking sites:

- ▶ Bebo
- ▶ Facebook
- ▶ Myspace
- ▶ Twitter
- ▶ LinkedIn (links professionals of all kinds).

▶ What exactly is 'blogging'?

It is said that Jorn Barger coined the term 'weblog' in 1997, by combining the words 'website' and 'logging'. 'Weblog' was then shortened to 'blog' by Peter Merholz in 1999, it is said. Blogging has grown extraordinarily quickly, and has become a new way of distributing news and other information, whether written, or in picture, audio or video form, and it has been embraced by millions of ordinary people, who feel they have something to say.

Here are just a few of the most popular sites you might like to start your blogging journey from:

Blogging websites

- Technorati.com
- Blogger.com
- Globalvoicesonline.org

- **Podcasts**

Most popular and well-known websites have podcasts as part of their resources. But there are also 'podcast directories', which are websites devoted entirely to podcasts. Here are some of the most popular:

- Podcast.com
- PodcastPickle.com
- Podnova.com

CHAPTER 14

Case study

Robert is being treated for stress and depression. He lacks energy and enthusiasm for anything these days, although he has a steady job as a joiner, and a good relationship with his wife and twin teenage sons, both of whom will be leaving home soon to go to university. He has few interests outside the family, and focusses most of his time and attention on his wife and the boys. He often finds himself brooding on the idea that he has wasted his life so far.

Look at the shorter version of Maslow's list of needs.

- Which of these are being met for Robert?
- Which of these might not be being met?
- Can you explain his feelings and depression?
- How motivated do you feel Robert is to meet his needs?
- Can you explain why Robert has this level of motivation?

Optional extras:

Appendix 2

Websites and contact details

POSTAL ADDRESSES

Centre for Mindfulness Research and Practice
Bangor University
School of Psychology
Dean St Building
Bangor University
Bangor LL57 1UT
Tel: 01248 382939
Fax: 01248 383982
E-mail: mindfulness@bangor.ac.uk
www.bangor.ac.uk/mindfulness

International Stress Management Association
PO Box 491
Bradley Stoke
Bristol BS34 9AH
www.isma.org.uk

MIND
15–19 Broadway
London E15 4BQ
Helpline: 0845 766 0163
www.mind.org.uk

Mind Cymru
3rd Floor
Quebec House
Castlebridge
5–19 Cowbridge Road East
Cardiff CF11 9AB
Tel: 029 2039 5123

National Association for Premenstrual Syndrome
41 Old Road East
Peckham
Kent TN12 5AP
Phone/fax 0870 777 2178
www.pms.org.uk
NHS Direct
Tel: 0845 4647

General advice on health matters.
No Panic
93 Brands Farm Way
Randley
Telford
Shropshire TF3 2JQ
E-mail: ceo@nopanic.org.uk
www.nopanic.org.uk
Free Helpline: 0808 808 0545, every day, 10am–10pm.

Information and support for panic attacks, phobias, obsessions.
Relaxation for Living Institute
1 Great Chapel St.
London W1F 8FA
Tel: 020 7439 4277

Samaritans
Tel: 08457 90 90 90 (24-hour)
E-mail: jo@samaritans.org
Scottish Association for Mental Health
Cumbrae House
15 Carlton Court
Glasgow G5 9JP
Tel: 0141 568 7000
E-mail: enquire@samh.org.uk
www.samh.org.uk

WEBSITES

▶ **Acupuncture**

www.acupuncture.com
www.relaxationexpert.co.uk/acupuncture.html

▶ **Alexander Technique**

www.alexandertechnique-itm.org

▶ **Alternative and complementary therapy links (general)**

British Holistic Medical Association: www.bhma.org

Federation of Holistic Therapists: www.fht.org.uk/home

The General Regulatory Council for Complementary Therapies: www.grcct.org/main

Internet Health Library: www.internethealthlibrary.com

Ireland's holistic directory: www.holisto.com

Research Council for Complementary Medicine: www.rccm.org.uk

The British Complementary Medicine Association: www.bcma.co.uk

▶ **Anger**

BBC: www.bbc.co.uk/health/emotional_health/mental_health/

BUPA: www.bupa.co.uk

NHS: www.nhs.uk/conditions/Anger-management/Pages/Introduction.aspx

http://www.smartmotorist.com/traffic-and-safety-guideline/road-rage-what-it-is-and-how-to-avoid-it.html

▶ **Biofeedback**

www.aleph1.co.uk

Biofeedback Foundation of Europe: www.bfe.org

www.futurehealth.org

www.holisticonline.com/biofeedback.htm

www.stresscheck.co.uk

▶ **Blogging**

www.blogcatalog.com

www.globalvoicesonline.com

www.technorati.com

▶ **Humour**

BBC: http://news.bbc.co.uk/1/hi/programmes/happiness_formula

European Network for Positive Psychology: www.enpp.eu

University of Pennsylvania: www.authentichappiness.sas.upenn.edu

www.siop.org/tip/Current/04warr.aspx

www.worlddatabaseofhappiness.eur.nl

www.pendulum.org

▶ **Massage therapy**

Chakra School Haad Rin: www.islandwebs.com/thailand/chakra.htm

ITEC: www.itecworld.co.uk

The Shiatsu Society (UK): www.shiatsu.org

www.massagetherapy.co.uk

▶ **Meditation**

www.meditationcenter.com

www.meditation-all-you-need.com/sounds.html

www.wildmind.org

▶ **Downloadable mandala images for immediate use or for colouring meditation**

www.cool-coloring-pages.com/mandalas.php

www.meaningofmandalas.com/mandala-coloring-pages.html

Or run a search for images of mandala for meditation – produces hundreds.

▶ **Mindfulness**

The Centre for Mindfulness Research and Practice within the School of Psychology, University of Wales Bangor: www.bangor.ac.uk/mindfulness

www.mindfulness.com

www.priory.com/psych/mindfulness.htm

► Music

www.kendavismusic.com/html/relaxation_music.html

www.relaxation-music.co.uk

www.silenciomusic.co.uk/index.htm

► NLP

Association of NLP: www.anlp.org

www.new-oceans.co.uk

www.NLPInfo.com

► NHS Choices

www.nhs.uk/Conditions

► Reflexology

www.reflexology-research.com

► Reiki

www.reiki.org

www.reikiliving.com

► Relaxation

www.health.discovery.com

www.imaginememedia.com

www.iserenity.com

www.natures-desktop.com

► Sleep

www.sleepcouncil.org.uk/sleep-advice

▶ Stress

Health and Safety Executive (HSE): www.hse.gov.uk

International Stress Management Association: www.isma.org.uk

www.workhealth.org

www.workstress.net

▶ T'ai Chi/Qigong

Chinese Wushu Research Institute GB: www.bigsky.uk.net/ index1.html (Provides t'ai chi/qigong instructors and advice to various interested bodies such as hospitals, colleges and schools)

www.qigonghealing.co.uk

www.taichifinder.co.uk

▶ Useful government funded websites for stress

www.breathingspacescotland

www.hse.gov.uk/stress

www.moodjuice.scot.nhs.uk/stress

Index